· T R O P H I E S ·

Intervention
PRACTICE BOOK
Grade 5

Harcourt

Orlando   Boston   Dallas   Chicago   San Diego

Visit *The Learning Site!*
www.harcourtschool.com

Printed in the United States of America

ISBN 0-15-326148-X

3 4 5 6 7 8 9 10 054 10 09 08 07 06 05 04 03

Table of Contents

Fluency Builder

authority	one	box
souvenir	asked	lines
incredible	were	swam
vow	with	fishing
commotion	knows	Ingrid
exhausted	really	poles
	again	game

1. Ingrid knows / an incredible amount / about fishing, / so she's an authority.

2. "Ingrid, / have you been fishing / again?" / asked Sam.

3. "I would have that huge one stuffed / as a souvenir / if I were you," / he said.

4. "Really?" / Ingrid asked / as she put her fishing lines / and poles / in her tackle box.

5. Suddenly, / there was a big commotion. / The fish started flopping, / knocking Ingrid's tackle box / to the ground.

6. With an incredible effort, / the exhausted fish flipped / and flopped / into the river / and swam away.

7. Ingrid and Sam made a vow / to play a game tomorrow, / instead of fishing.

Harcourt

Name _____

A Fish Tale

Do what the sentences tell you.

June _____

_____

1. Find Dan. He has a *D* on his cap. Write *Dan* on the line by him.
2. Find Mike. He has an *M* on his cap. Write *Mike* on the line by him.
3. Dan has no rod to catch fish with. Make a fishing rod in his hand.
4. Mike likes to fish with a stick and a string. Make a pole for him to fish with.
5. Find June. Make a line from one of her hands to the other.
6. Then draw a fish on the line.
7. Make five stripes on the fish.
8. Make some waves on the lake.
9. Draw a big pine on a sand dune by Dan.
10. Find the ring of stones. Make a blaze in it.
11. Make a plume of smoke going up from the blaze.
12. Find the pup. Make a mat for the pup to nap on.

Write a word from above that has the same vowel sound and spelling pattern as each word below.

13. tune _____ 15. haze _____

14. bike _____ 16. joke _____

Name _____

A Fish Tale

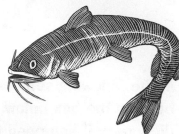

Write a sentence in each box below to help you summarize
"A Fish Tale." Be sure to write the events in the correct order.

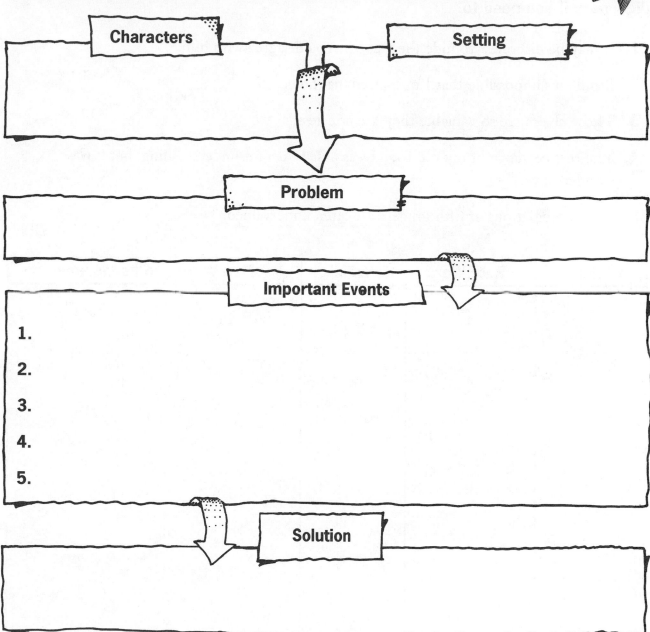

Characters

Setting

Problem

Important Events

1.

2.

3.

4.

5.

Solution

Now write a one-sentence summary of the story.

_____

_____

Prefixes and Suffixes

In the following sentences underline the words that include prefixes or suffixes or both. In the box below, write the parts of each word and the word's meaning. Use a dictionary if you need to.

1. It may be dishonest to hide the fact that you disagree with him.

2. I think it's impossible that I misplaced that book.

3. Those chairs are so valuable they are priceless.

4. The reappearance of my old friend was based on a misunderstanding, but it was wonderful.

5. The contributions of fifth graders are often undervalued.

Prefix	Root Word	Suffix	New Word and Its Meaning

Harcourt

Fluency Builder

tread	when	shed
moss	coming	tree
sternly	knew	scent
compose	hear	creek
exaggerate	then	west
quiver	put	breeze
	was	feel

1. When he had lost his quiver, / he was heading west / toward the creek.

2. He knew / that his father would sternly punish him / if he came home without it.

3. He searched / around the moss covered / tree stumps.

4. He had promised himself / that he would not shed a tear, / but he could feel them / streaming down his face.

5. He had to compose himself, / or he would never find / his quiver.

6. Then the breeze / brought the scent / of something / unfamiliar.

7. Someone was coming. / He could hear / the soft tread / of a boy.

8. With exaggerated movements, / the boy / carefully / put the quiver / on the ground.

The Quiver

Write the word that makes the sentence tell about the picture.

1. Janet has a _____ finch named Flute.

            vest   pet   jet

2. She puts _____ in Flute's dish.

         seeds   feet   weeds

3. Flute likes to hit her bell and _____.

                   keys   honey   jockey

4. She _____ a nice tune when it's time for lunch.

     tweets   jeeps   beets

5. Sometimes Janet must _____ Flute's home.

          leap   clean   deal

6. At bedtime, Flute _____ on her swing.

        weeds   speeds   sleeps

7. Flute _____ to like her home.

      speeds   seems   bees

The Quiver

Complete the sequence chart about "The Quiver." Write a sentence in each box. The first one is done for you.

Event 1:

Will finds a quiver and gets lost while looking for more things.

Event 2:

Event 3:

Event 4:

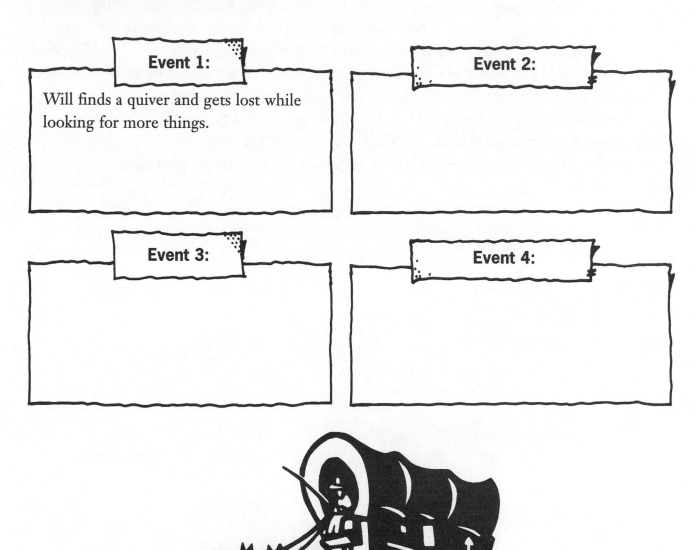

Narrative Elements

Read the story, and fill in the blanks.

Jill and Jeri planted a vegetable garden in Jill's backyard. They found a corner of the yard where Mom used to plant flowers. Mom said the girls could use that section for their garden. After they planted six rows of beans, two rows of tomatoes, and one row of lettuce, they kept the plants watered and pulled out the weeds. After a couple of weeks, the beans and tomatoes were growing well, but the lettuce was only one inch high. They inspected the leaves, and there were no bugs on the lettuce. They explained the problem to Dad. He wasn't sure what the problem was but told them he saw a rabbit in the yard the other day. Jill and Jeri decided to build a small fence around the lettuce to keep the rabbit out of the garden.

Characters: _____

Setting: _____

Problem or Conflict: _____

Solution: _____

_____

Harcourt

Fluency Builder

audition	fill	hall
sonata	look	halt
accompaniment	was	wall
accompanist	one	waltz
grimaced	they	called
simultaneously	began	Aldo
	fill	
	came	

1. Jean looked / at the clock / on the wall.

2. The audition / was scheduled to begin / at ten o'clock.

3. Jean planned / to play a waltz / for the audition.

4. Miss Small called on students / to audition / one at a time.

5. Aldo nodded to the accompanist, / a pianist, / and they began to play / simultaneously.

6. The notes of a sonata / filled the hall.

7. When Aldo suddenly jumped up, / the accompaniment came to a halt.

8. Aldo grimaced / because one of his cello strings / had broken.

The Audition

Read the story. Circle the words with the vowel sound you hear in *salt*, *hall*, or *stalk*.

Walt is now six feet tall.	He needs to walk to the mall to get longer pants.	He calls Beth to make a plan: "I'll get you a malt if you come with me to the mall."
Then Beth talks. She tells Walt that the baseball game has ended. "I'll meet you at the stone wall next to the lake at three."	Walt hangs up. When he walks outside, the crisp fall breeze makes him smile.	Walt meets Beth at the stone wall at three. He gets her a malt at a shop in the mall. For himself, he gets a frozen treat with walnuts.

Circle and write the word that best completes each sentence.

1. Walt is not _____. small   wall   call

2. He has to get pants at the _____. wall   mall   hall

3. He plans to get there by _____. walking   talking   balking

4. He _____ Beth to see if she'll go. stalls   halls   calls

5. He tells her he'll get her a _____. malt   salt   walnut

6. They _____ about a plan to meet. talk   walk   stall

7. Walt likes the _____ breeze. fall   tall   salt

8. He asks for a treat with _____. walnuts   salt   stalks

Harcourt

The Audition

Write a sentence in each box below to help you summarize "The Audition." Be sure to write the events in the correct order.

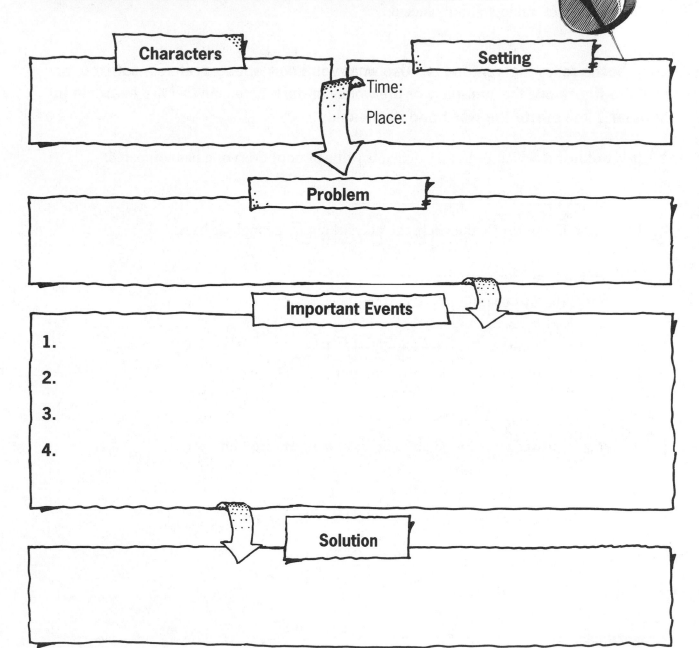

Characters

Setting

Time:

Place:

Problem

Important Events

1.

2.

3.

4.

Solution

Now write a one-sentence summary of the story.

_____

_____

Prefixes, Suffixes, and Roots

A prefix is a word part added to the beginning of a root. A suffix is a word part added to the end of a root. Prefixes and suffixes change the meaning of roots. Knowing the parts of a word can help you understand its meaning.

Look at the following sentences. Use what you know about prefixes, suffixes, and roots to figure out the meaning of the words in dark type. Follow the example in number 1 to rewrite the word and its meaning.

1. It is **unknown** which of the participants will win until everyone has competed.

    un + known = not known

2. Each time Kevin threw the stick, the **playful** puppy brought it back.

    _____

3. Karen had the **impossible** job of cleaning her room in less than an hour.

    _____

4. Laura was **envious** of my success on the test.

    _____

5. The movie **preview** promised an exciting new adventure film.

    _____

6. A bear's **fondness** for honey can lead to a lot of bee stings.

    _____

7. The book Kelly read was **nonfiction**.

    _____

8. New curtains would really **brighten** this room.

    _____

Harcourt

Fluency Builder

ridiculed	wanted	smart
dignity	new	career
counsel	teacher	Barbara
potential	grandma	started
inspire	sat	
correspondence	she	
mentor	talk	
	with	
	their	

1. Jane's correspondence / with her grandma / was by e-mail.

2. Barbara Jordan was / a smart career woman / with dignity and confidence.

3. Jane's classmates were inspired / by the talk / she gave / on the career / of Barbara Jordan.

4. Barbara Jordan was not ridiculed / by her peers. / They counseled her / to run for the U.S. Congress.

5. Later, / Barbara Jordan started a new career / as a teacher. / She was / a mentor and guide / to her students.

6. Wilma Downs feels / that her granddaughter / has as much potential / as Barbara Jordan.

7. Barbara Jordan wanted / to inspire others / to achieve their potential.

8. The class / liked Jane's talk so much that / she asked her grandma / to talk to the class.

Name _____

Lessons from
Barbara Jordan

Write the word that answers each riddle.

1. I have the *ar* sound you hear in *part*.
   I am driven along streets. What am I? _____

                   cart   plane   car

2. I have the same *ar* sound as in *charm*.
   I am a sweet treat. What am I? _____

                tarp   tart   cake

3. I have the same *ar* sound as in *card*.
   I am a fish. What am I? _____

            shark   sharp   cod

4. I have the *ar* sound you hear in *harp*.
   I am made of glass, and I have a lid. What am I? _____

                 glass   jar   cart

5. I have the same *ar* sound as in *yarn*.
   I shine in the dark. What am I? _____

            star   mark   moon

6. I have the same *ar* sound as in *lark*.
   Sheep can sleep in me. What am I? _____

              pen   barn   bark

7. I have the same *ar* sound as in *tar*.
   I am not close to you. What am I? _____

             far   mark   fast

8. I have the same *ar* sound as in *harm*.
   I am what you do when you stop a car and get out.

   What am I? _____

        jump   start   park

9. I have the same *ar* sound as in *spark*.
   You can toss me at a target. What am I? _____

             chart   dart   ball

10. I have the *ar* sound you hear in *smart*.
    You shop for milk and eggs in me. What am I? _____

            parsnip   market   snack

Harcourt

Lessons from Barbara Jordan

Write one sentence in each box below to summarize the ideas presented on those pages about Barbara Jordan.

Pages 30–31

Main Idea:

Pages 32–33

Main Idea:

Pages 34–35

Main Idea:

Now write a one-sentence summary of the selection.

_____

Harcourt

Make Judgments

Read the passage, then answer the questions below.

Just before dinner, Mr. Jones and his three children went for a walk in the woods. Mrs. Jones told them dinner would be ready in an hour and to be back in time to eat. As they walked down the path, they noticed some birds and many flowers. Soon, one of the children saw a fawn. The baby deer could be seen in a grassy area and seemed to be looking at them. They moved carefully toward the deer. It started to scamper away, and they followed it. They soon lost the trail of the fawn, and when they looked around, they knew they were lost. They began to search for the way home but could not find it. By accident, Mr. Jones and the children found the trail and ran home. Mrs. Jones was standing in the doorway with a frown on her face and her arms folded.

1. Which of the following is a valid judgment?

   a. Mr. Jones and the children forgot the time.

   b. Mr. Jones and the children did not want to be late for dinner.

   c. Mr. Jones and the children did not like wildlife.

   d. Mr. Jones and the children felt bad about not catching the fawn.

2. Which of the following is a valid judgment?

   a. Mr. Jones and the children were on time for dinner.

   b. Dinner included cold salads and sandwiches.

   c. The dinner Mrs. Jones had cooked was delicious.

   d. Mr. Jones and the children would have to explain why they were late.

Harcourt

Fluency Builder

revolution	have	paid
plunged	his	that
ravine	found	main
mocking	fine	land
determination	care	paint
condolences	art	sand
	would	
	said	

1. Pablo paid Diego his condolences / when he found out / that Diego had to leave / their fine land / and sail to Mexico.

2. When Diego talked / about how he had to paint their homeland, / Pablo said in a mocking tone, / "They do not care for art there."

3. However, / Diego showed much determination.

4. When he got to Mexico, / he plunged into his job / and painted jungle ravines / filled with vines.

5. Much of Diego's art / spoke of the revolution / of his land.

6. He invited Pablo / to come and see / one of his paintings.

7. Pablo told Diego / that his painting was / a "genuine piece of art."

8. Finally, / Diego's work / was made public, / and everyone grew / to appreciate his art.

Painting My Homeland

Read the story. Then choose the best answer for each question. Circle the letter for that answer.

Clayton looked down the tracks for the midday train. It was always late. As he waited, he started daydreaming about Spain. He was traveling there next week with his wife, Gail.

"Please," said a man who had a little boy with him, interrupting his daydream, "where can we catch the train to Main Street?"

"You can stay here with me. I'm catching that train, too," Clayton responded.

"Good," the man said. Then the man spoke to the boy in Spanish.

Clayton said, "Excuse me for asking, but are you from Spain?"

"Yes, I am!" the man said. He looked puzzled.

"Let me explain," Clayton said. "My wife and I are visiting Spain next week. We are very pleased to be going. The trip is always on my brain!"

The man smiled. "Spain is hot this time of year," he said. "What are your travel plans?"

"We hope to visit some of the historic landmarks, go sailing, and play in the sun. It will be fantastic!"

1 What was Clayton looking for?
 A the midday bus
 B a cab on Main Street
 C the evening train
 D the midday train

2 What did he do while he waited?
 F He daydreamed about his trip.
 G He clapped his hands.
 H He played a game.
 J He filed his nails.

3 What are Clayton and Gail going to do?
 A wait for rain
 B travel to Spain
 C sail to Paris
 D pay for pancakes

4 The man from Spain
 F started daydreaming, too.
 G asked Clayton about the mail.
 H spoke in Spanish.
 J was afraid of cats.

5 What was the man looking for?
 A a cab to Main Street
 B a bag of grain
 C the train Clayton was waiting for
 D a needle in a haystack

6 Why did Clayton ask the man if he was from Spain?
 F He wanted to explain why the train was late.
 G The man spoke in Spanish.
 H He wanted to say a joke.
 J The man had paid for his Spanish lessons.

Harcourt

Painting My Homeland

Complete the sequence chart about "Painting My Homeland." Write a sentence in each box.

Event 1:

Diego decides he must return home to Mexico.

Event 2:

Event 3:

Event 4:

Event 5:

Event 6:

Now use the information from the boxes to write a one-sentence summary of the selection.

_____

_____

Narrative Elements

Read the passage and then answer the questions.

Marty and Ben were brothers who had just moved with their mother and father from New York to live on a farm in Ohio. Each boy liked to help others and made sure games at school were played fairly. One day when a bully started a fight with the pitcher of a game, Marty and Ben were there to break it up before the fighters got in trouble. The pitcher became a fast friend after that. When Fred forgot his lunch, they shared their food with him. They were kind to people and animals alike.

One day when they were going home after school, they took a shortcut through Mr. Blade's fields and past his barns. They didn't know why, but the back wall of the pig barn was so close to the fence that a boy of twelve could barely squeeze through. That day, though, you wouldn't have wanted to try to get through that opening because there was a big sow stuck in there, and she wasn't happy. Marty and Ben worked together to free up some of the boards in the fence, and the sow came loose. She ranted and snorted for a good fifteen minutes. By the time the boys got home, Mr. Blade had called to thank the boys for their help. The boys' parents were very proud of Marty and Ben.

1. As the story begins, the setting is

   a. in the sixth grade classroom.

   b. on the playground at school in Ohio.

   c. in the lunchroom.

   d. at home in New York.

2. On their way home after school, what is the setting?

   a. a corn field

   b. near Mr. Blade's chicken coop

   c. behind the pig barn

   d. on the road

3. What is the theme of this story? _____

_____

4. How do the characters' actions help you identify the theme? _____

_____

_____

_____

Fluency Builder

lineup	ball	down
ace	someone	after
error	that	boast
artificial	would	billboard
control tower	because	groaned
dedicated	star	
	lost	
	hard	
	couldn't	

1. Roberto Clemente / was a dedicated ball player.

2. He promised himself / that he would play hard / for his team.

3. People groaned / that the Pirates / couldn't beat the ace lineup / of the Orioles.

4. The billboard / at the ballpark read / "Home of the Orioles."

5. Clemente, / the star player, / said that was an error. / His team / was going to win!

6. Although he was one / of the best baseball players, / Clemente didn't boast.

7. Clemente gave money to someone / who needed artificial legs.

8. In 1972, / Roberto Clemente lost his life. / The control tower / didn't see / that the plane he rode in / was about to go down.

9. After he lost his life, / Clemente's fans dedicated / a statue to him.

Name _____

The Pirate Hero

**Read the story. Circle all the words that have the short sound of the vowel *o*.
Draw a line under all the words that have the long sound of the vowel *o*.**

Rob, Kim, and Joan went camping near a lake. Joan steered the boat into the bank with confidence. Rob jumped out and tugged the boat up onto the rocks. "What a mess!" Joan said as she got out. Wind had whipped up the waves on the lake. Her pants legs were wet. Her socks were soaked.

"Let's unload this stuff," Kim said. Rob grabbed the sleeping bags and pitched them up onto the bank. Then he grabbed his rod and reel.

"I'll catch a fine fish!" he boasted. "We can roast it on some coals." Then off he went. Kim moaned. She did not care much for ordinary lake fish. But Joan had said that one must make sacrifices when camping.

"Well, fish it is," Kim said. "I'll put my coat on and get some sticks." Joan helped her. They made a hot blaze. Rob came back in a bit. He held a line of gleaming fish. They roasted the fish on a grate on the coals. They made hot toast to have with it. Then they ate. Kim said with surprise, "This is the best fish I've ever had, Rob! Thanks!"

Now write the long *o* word or the short *o* word that best completes each sentence.

1. _____ said that one must make sacrifices when camping.

2. Joan, Rob, and Kim got to the camping spot in a _____.

3. Joan's pants and _____ got wet on the trip.

4. Wind-whipped waves had _____ her.

5. Rob grabbed his fishing _____ when they got to the site.

6. He _____ that he'd catch some fine fish.

7. Kim _____ at the prospect of eating lake fish.

8. They _____ the fish.

Harcourt

Name _____

The Pirate Hero

Complete the sequence chart about "The Pirate Hero." Write a sentence in each box.

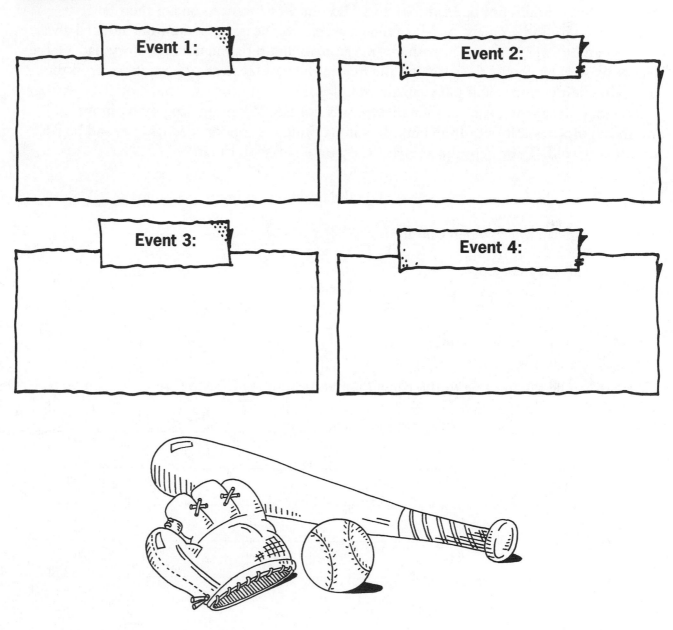

Event 1:	Event 2:
Event 3:	Event 4:

Now use the information from the boxes to write a one-sentence summary of the selection.

_____

_____

Harcourt

Draw Conclusions

Read the paragraph. Then answer the questions below.

Some animals should not be kept together. Max and Rory went to one of their favorite nature areas to find animals. As Max found a green frog near the pond, Rory noticed a warty toad on an old tree stump. They caught the animals and took them home. Rory had a large fish tank, so they placed the toad and the frog in the tank. Instead of putting water in the tank, they left it empty and put a small bowl of water in one corner. They noticed the frog stayed away from the toad but thought that was normal. When the frog didn't move anymore, they took it out of the tank. In a short time, the frog opened its eyes and began to move around. They kept the animals in separate tanks after that.

1. Which is the best conclusion based on the information in the paragraph?

   a. Frogs fall asleep when captured.

   b. Toads may eat frogs.

   c. Toads give off a toxic scent that is poisonous to other animals.

   d. Frogs need water to live.

2. Explain how you came to the conclusion you chose for Question 1.

_____

_____

_____

_____

Harcourt

Fluency Builder

diligence
plodded
bountiful
destiny
assured
entrusted

what
through
sun
help
rain
fine
grass
tree

grow
rainbow
snow
know
slow
glow

1. The Sun rewarded the Rain / for her diligence / with helping the trees / to grow.

2. The people plodded / down the road / covered with snow.

3. The Rain assured the Snow / that the people needed her / to help the grass / to grow.

4. The Rain took credit / for the bountiful harvest / of fine wheat and oats.

5. The Rain and the Snow / entrusted the Sun / with an important decision.

6. At first / the Sun was slow / to take sides. / "I must know / what you can do," / she said.

7. It is the destiny / of both the Rain and the Snow / to be important.

8. The glow / of the Sun / through the rain / made a rainbow.

The Rain and the Snow

Do what the sentences tell you to do.

1. Find three cats in a row. Add a cat to the row.
2. Make a bowl for the cats.
3. Make a tree growing next to the pond.
4. Put a crow up in the tree.
5. Show a leaf blowing away from the tree.
6. Put a dog in the shade below the tree.
7. Put an X on the rowboat next to the pond.
8. A boy named Rob owns the boat. Show who Rob is by making an *R* on his hat.
9. Oh, no, it's snowing! Make some snow falling.
10. Make a pile of six snowballs in Rob's boat.
11. Make Rob hold a paddle to row the boat with.
12. Find the fish. Then make an arrow that shows Rob the way to the pond.
13. Show some of the bubbles the fish are blowing.
14. Find one cat that's not in a row of cats. Make a small bowl for it to eat out of.

Now circle all the words that have the long sound of the vowel *o* spelled *ow*.

Harcourt

Name _____

The Rain and the Snow

Complete the sequence chart about "The Rain and the Snow."

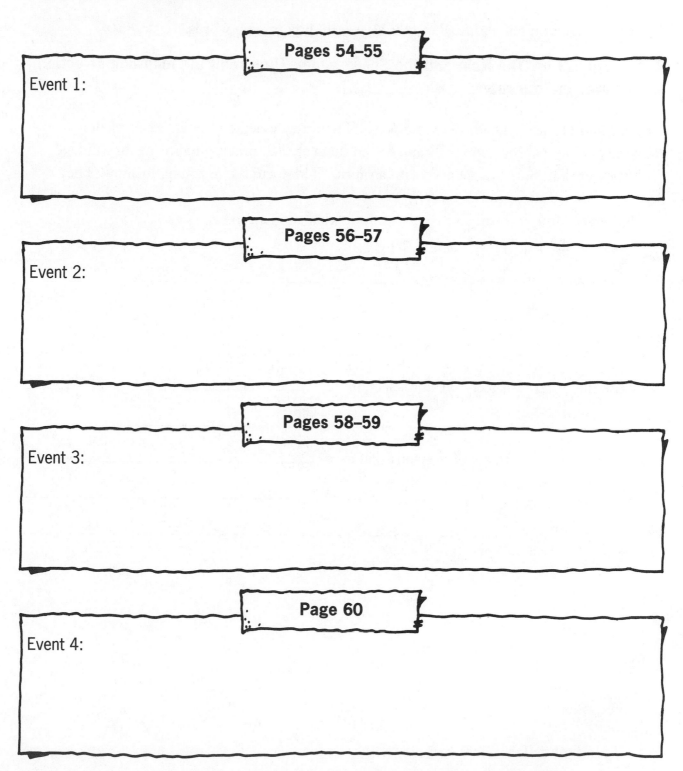

Pages 54–55

Event 1:

Pages 56–57

Event 2:

Pages 58–59

Event 3:

Page 60

Event 4:

Summarize and Paraphrase

To **summarize** you retell what you have read in a shorter form.

To **paraphrase** you tell about what you have read in your own words.

Read page 59 of "The Rain and the Snow" again. Then read the following selection and answer the questions.

Kids and moms and dads peered outside. Then they raced outdoors. They made snowmen. They packed snowballs and tossed them at each other, giggling as they did.

"Look at that, Sun," said Snow with a smirk. "These guys love rolling in snow. They'd be really upset if there weren't any."

Rain and Snow stopped and waited to hear what sun had to say.

Is this a summary or a paraphrase? _____

How do you know? _____

_____

Now use the other skill to retell this selection. _____

_____

How is this different from the previous skill used? _____

_____

_____

Harcourt

Fluency Builder

headquarters	was	snowstorm
positions	were	morning
handlers	step	door
tangle	out	transporting
pace	along	
	help	
	dog	
	early	
	after	
	from	
	couldn't	

1. The medical headquarters / was located / in Anchorage, Alaska.

2. The obstacles / to transporting the medicine / were incredible.

3. Day after day, / the medicine traveled nonstop, / passing from one musher / to the next.

4. When a snowstorm hit, / the huskies couldn't keep pace.

5. They stepped out of their positions / and tangled their lines.

6. There were no extra dog handlers / along to help.

7. In the early morning darkness, / Dr. Welch heard a rap / at his door.

8. The race for life / was won.

Name _____

Race for Life on the Iditarod Trail

Circle and write the word that makes sense in the sentence.

1. Dogsledding is a hard and demanding _____.

            spot   sport   spoke

2. Sled drivers, called mushers, must travel in bad _____.

            storms   stoves   stomps

3. Huskies are _____ to the job of pulling sleds.

          barn   born   bond

4. On the trail, sled dogs sleep in

_____ made of snow.

  farms   forests   forts

5. Thick coats help the dogs sleep well on a _____ made
of snow.   **floor   flute   flock**

6. A lot of sled dog breeders make their homes in the far _____.

           north   nor   not

7. The musher must keep _____ within the team of dogs.

        odder   order   orchard

8. A musher must have a job _____ each dog and must teach the
dog to do it well.   **fort   far   for**

9. A mush team's day often starts early in

the _____.

moon   mound   morning

10. But sled dogs do an _____ job, and they like the job
they do.   **important   impostor   immortal**

11. The people of Nome, Alaska, will never _____ how dogsled
teams saved lives one winter.   **forget   forlorn   forts**

Harcourt

Race for Life on the Iditarod Trail

Complete the sequence chart about "Race for Life on the Iditarod Trail." Write a sentence in each box.

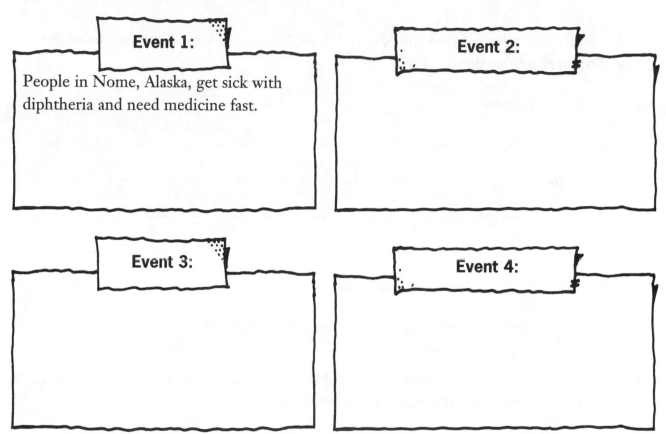

Event 1:

People in Nome, Alaska, get sick with diphtheria and need medicine fast.

Event 2:

Event 3:

Event 4:

Now use the information from the boxes to write a one-sentence summary of the entire selection.

_____

_____

_____

Harcourt

Draw Conclusions

Fill in the blanks.

To **draw conclusions** about a selection, you need to notice the story details and draw from your own experience.

Think about "Race for Life on the Iditarod Trail." List the important details of the story. The first one is done for you.

1. Children have diphtheria.

2. _____

3. _____

4. _____

5. _____

6. _____

7. _____

Now list your personal experiences that relate to this story. Focus on doing things in bad weather and how people react in an emergency.

1. _____

2. _____

3. _____

What conclusions can you draw about the people in this story?

1. These mushers are able to work very hard, because they are champions.

2. _____

Harcourt

Fluency Builder

resembled	**watch**	**adore**
retired	**over**	**four**
snort	**family**	**oars**
harness	**fish**	**bore**
disengage	**made**	**chore**
bulk	**from**	**wore**
pointedly		**roar**

1. The rhythm of the oars / bore them / over the waves.

2. Fishing isn't a chore / for the four family members.

3. Little Elinore / wore her harness / over her life jacket's bulk.

4. Suze said pointedly, / "I'm going to catch more fish / than you!"

5. When dad disengaged the motor, / it made a snort / and went still.

6. One more wiggling fish / had retired from swimming.

7. The fish resembled / a little man with long whiskers.

8. I watched the sun set / over the sea / we adore.

Fishing for Four

Read the story. Circle all the words that have the vowel sound heard in *more*.

Norm, the chimp, had lots of chores to do. He had to feed his pet boar. He had to cut some boards to fix the boar's pen. He had to stack the oars in the shed. Then there were ripe gourds to pick and store in the attic. "I'm bored with this routine," Norm complained. "What will it matter if I skip the chores just one time?" Norm went up to his bed. He started to snore. Meanwhile, the hungry boar left its pen to explore. When Norm woke up, he stared in disbelief! What a mess! The boar had gobbled up all the gourds. It had run over the oars and smashed them to bits. "What more?" Norm wailed as he ran to the shed. The boar was there, munching on apple cores. There were no more apples in the bin.

Circle and write the word that best completes each sentence.

1. Norm skipped his _____.   **store**   **boar**   **chores**

2. His pet _____ got out of its pen.   **gourd**   **goat**   **boar**

3. Norm's mistake was in getting _____.   **bored**   **poured**   **sore**

4. He was supposed to pick the _____.   **corn**   **gourds**   **cores**

5. He was supposed to stack the _____.   **cores**   **gourds**   **oars**

6. He was supposed to cut the _____.   **more**   **boards**   **corn**

7. It was not smart of Norm to_____ all day.   **snore**   **core**   **soar**

8. Now he has a bigger job than he had _____.   **implore**   **before**   **ignore**

Harcourt

Fishing for Four

Complete the sequence chart about "Fishing for Four."
Write a sentence or two in each box. The first one is done for you.

Event 1 **(Pages 70–71)**	**Event 2** **(Pages 72–73)**
Dad rows the three kids out to the big boat for a day of fishing for crab bait. The two older kids will compete to see how many fish they can catch.	
Event 3 **(Pages 74–75)**	**Event 4** **(Page 76)**

Now use the information from the boxes to write a one-sentence summary of the story.

_____

_____

Harcourt

Summarize and Paraphrase

When you **summarize** a story, you briefly retell the main idea using facts and details from the story. When you **paraphrase** a story, you tell the story, but use your own words.

> "Get on board, kids," said Dad. Elinore, who is just four, had to sit on the floor of the boat. Suze and I were gratified to be able to sit on the board at the back. Dad pulled on the oars in a slow rhythm. When we got into the big boat, the motor emitted a roar as it started up.
>
> We were helping our dad catch some fish to use as crab bait. We like going fishing with him.
>
> "I'm going to catch more fish than you," said Suze. She and I like to compete.
>
> Dad calculated. "If we can fill four bushel baskets, that will do it," he said.
>
> Elinore is an innocent little kid. She didn't know that Suze and I were having a contest. She ignored her fishing line.

Dad takes his three children fishing to get crab bait, and the two older ones compete to get the most fish while the little one doesn't pay any attention to fishing.

Read the sentence above in bold type. Is this a summary or a paraphrase?

_____

How do you know that? _____

_____

Fluency Builder

overcome	away	worked
forlorn	could	fur
pitched	watch	churning
vainer	over	search
gorged	lost	turned
abalone	without	gurgling
lair	knew	

1. Lani could not go / with the men / to search / for abalone.

2. She felt lost and forlorn / as she watched / the men paddle away.

3. Kalo said / that Lani could hide in his canoe, / and she was overcome / with joy.

4. Kalo and Lani passed / by the lair / of the seals / and watched a vainer seal / lick his fur all over.

5. The other seals / gorged themselves / on fish.

6. Suddenly, / a fierce storm / turned over the canoes / of the other men.

7. Lani and Kalo worked together / to paddle through / the churning water / and turn over the flipped canoes.

8. All of the men knew / they would have been lost / in the gurgling waves / without Lani's help.

Name _____

Raindrop in the Sun

Write the word that answers each riddle.

1. I have the same vowel sound and spelling as in *pearl*.

I am a planet. What am I? _____
Earth   earn   Saturn

2. I have the same vowel sound and spelling as in *turn*.

I am a color. What am I? _____
purse   purple   teal

3. I have the same vowel sound and spelling as in *bird*.

Girls dress up in me. What am I? _____
twirl   dress   skirt

4. I have the same vowel sound and spelling as in *herd*.

I am a kind of fish. What am I? _____
perch   search   fern

5. I have the same vowel sound and spelling as in *work*.

I mean the opposite of better. What am I? _____
woods   worms   worse

6. I have the same vowel sound and spelling as in the first syllable of *early*.

I mean "to have an earnest desire." What am I? _____
yearn   hope   learn

7. I have the same vowel sound and spelling as in *burn*.

I mean "silly or senseless." What am I? _____
turned   absurd   odd

8. I have the same vowel sound and spelling as in *dirt*.

I am a kind of tree. What am I? _____
birch   maple   shirt

Harcourt

Name _____

Raindrop in the Sun

Complete the chart to retell the story.

Cause	Effect
Moro told Lani she was too weak to paddle a _____.	Kalo told Lani to meet him by the cave's _____. He hid her in his boat.
raft canoe rowboat	**entrance side back**
Kalo and Lani _____ well as a team.	Kalo and Lani _____ a lot of abalones.
worked played hid	**cleaned ate gathered**
A _____ storm came up. Lani and Kalo saved the men.	Moro _____ up and gave a speech. He called Lani a hero.
soft fierce winter	**drove flew strode**

Now write a sentence that summarizes the story.

_____

_____

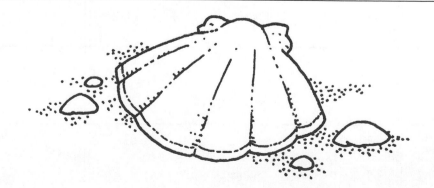

Narrative Elements

Read the story. Fill in the Narrative Elements chart below with information from the story.

Mr. and Mrs. Sanson took their family to the beach. They had two sons: Bret, a fifth grader, and Kirk, a first grader. After they found a good spot, they put down their blankets and set up an umbrella. It wasn't long before Kirk started to build sand houses and roads for his metal cars to drive on. He brought three of his favorite cars to the beach. Bret seemed interested in electricity and magnetism and brought a few books to read. At noon the family had lunch, and afterward, when Kirk returned to his sand houses and cars, they were not there. Someone must have driven over them by accident. He searched with his hands and found one car. When his family saw what had happened, Bret remembered he had a horseshoe magnet in the car. He got it, and Kirk and Bret used it to find the cars in the sand.

NARRATIVE ELEMENTS

Characters	
Setting	
Plot: Problem or Conflict	
Plot: Solution	
Theme	

Harcourt

Fluency Builder

eons	birthday	both
peninsula	his	over
scurried	will	we
multitude	started	find
plenitude	help	Jason
pondered	change	ago
	were	become

1. Eons ago / manatees scurried / over the land / like other mammals.

2. There were a multitude / of manatees /on both sides / of the Florida peninsula.

3. Manatees help / keep the plenitude / of weeds / from choking Florida waterways.

4. Jason pondered / the manatee model / his grandpa gave him / for a birthday gift.

5. Jason wanted to help change / the fate faced / by manatees.

6. Over time / manatees will become extinct / if we don't help them.

7. If everyone started to help, / then multitudes / of manatees would always swim / in Florida waterways.

8. Jason plans / to find a club / on the Web / or start one / of his own.

Name

The Gift of the Manatee

Circle the letter in front of the sentence that tells about the picture.

1 **A** Willy pets the lion.

   B Willy stands behind the zebra.

   C Willy uses the broom.

   D Willy rolls under the zebra.

2 **F** April hides the tomatoes in her apron.

   G April stirs the tomatoes with a ladle.

   H April holds the tomatoes in the crate.

   J April picks the tomatoes from her home.

3 **A** Emily is a pilot in the Navy.

   B Emily cares for lions at the wildlife park.

   C Emily explores volcanoes.

   D Emily has a program on the radio.

4 **F** Ruby's baby sister finds a tiny radio.

   G Ruby's baby sister rides an old bike.

   H Ruby's baby sister winds the funny clock.

   J Ruby's baby sister finds an acorn.

5 **A** Ty and Mona dry their hands on their aprons.

   B Ty and Mona don't like the flavor of tuna.

   C Ty and Mona try to keep dry in the rain.

   D Ty and Mona think the lake is cold.

6 **F** Peter makes the ball fly over the goal posts.

   G Peter finds a spider behind the piano.

   H Peter grinds the corn with a stone.

   J Peter strolls by the cargo door.

Name _____

The Gift of the Manatee

Write one sentence in each box below to show what you learned about the manatee.

Pages 86–87

What does Jason learn about where the manatee lives, and where it may be going?

Page 88

How did manatees become water animals?

Pages 90–91

What does Jason learn about the dangers to the manatee, and what does he decide to do about that?

Now use the information in the boxes to write a one-sentence summary of the selection.

_____

_____

Prefixes, Suffixes, and Roots

Fill in the blanks to tell about prefixes, suffixes, and roots.

The _____ of a word carries the word's basic meaning.

A _____ is added to the beginning of a word.

A _____ is added to the end of a word.

Both _____ and _____ change the
meaning of the root or root word.

**Read the chart. Study the word parts and their meanings. Then answer the
questions below.**

Prefix		Root		Suffix	
in-	"not"	vis	"see"	-ible	"able"
		aud	"hear"	-ation	"the act of"
		dict	"speak"		

What is the root in the word <u>visible</u>? _____

What is the meaning of the word <u>visible</u>? _____

How is the word <u>audible</u> like the word <u>visible</u>? _____

What is the meaning of the word <u>audible</u>? What is the meaning of the word <u>inaudible</u>?

_____

What is <u>dictation</u>? _____

**Use the word parts in the chart to form words that you know, and write them on the
lines. Then write the meanings of the words.**

_____   _____

_____   _____

Harcourt

Fluency Builder

dwindled	in	showers
tinder	park	spout
policy	fire	ground
canopy	went	however
embers	fell	out
geyser	snow	
veered	rain	
	many	

1. Geysers spout / at Yellowstone National Park.

2. In 1988 / Yellowstone became / as dry as tinder.

3. It is the park's policy / to let fires burn / until rain showers end them.

4. Fierce winds / made the fires veer / this way and that.

5. The forest canopy / went up in flames.

6. Red-hot embers / fell to the ground / and started more fires.

7. In September, / snow and rain / caused the flames to dwindle / and finally go out.

8. Through the winter, / the land did not offer much to eat, / however, / many animals survived.

Harcourt

Name _____

Flowers After the Flames

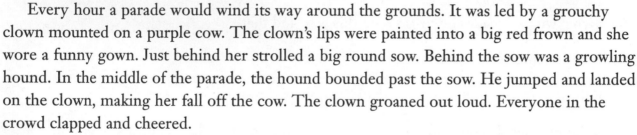

Read the story, and circle all the words with the same vowel sound as in *pound* and *now*.

Last summer a traveling carnival came to town. For several days, we heard the pounding of hammers and the humming of drills.

A big crowd came to it the first day. Inside the grounds the visitors found lots of rides and games. There was a Ferris wheel that went around and around. There was a winding slide connected to a big tower.

Every hour a parade would wind its way around the grounds. It was led by a grouchy clown mounted on a purple cow. The clown's lips were painted into a big red frown and she wore a funny gown. Just behind her strolled a big round sow. Behind the sow was a growling hound. In the middle of the parade, the hound bounded past the sow. He jumped and landed on the clown, making her fall off the cow. The clown groaned out loud. Everyone in the crowd clapped and cheered.

Now write the word with the same vowel sound as in *pound* and *now* that best completes each sentence.

1. The carnival came to _____ last summer.

2. The slide was connected to a _____.

3. The first day a big _____ attended the carnival.

4. Every hour a parade wound its way _____ the grounds.

5. A _____ clown led the parade.

6. The clown wore a funny gown and had a big red _____.

7. A sow and a _____ were behind her.

8. The hound made the clown fall off a purple _____.

Harcourt

Flowers After the Flames

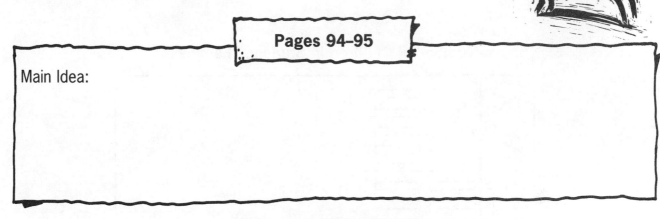

Write one sentence in each box below to summarize the main idea presented on the given pages.

Pages 94–95

Main Idea:

Pages 96–97

Main Idea:

Pages 98–99

Main Idea:

Now write a one-sentence summary of "Flowers After the Flames."

_____

_____

Harcourt

Graphic Aids

Graphic aids that are used in books and newspapers include photographs, charts, diagrams, illustrations and maps. Graphic aids can help one understand information that is difficult or complex.

Number of Children in Students' Families

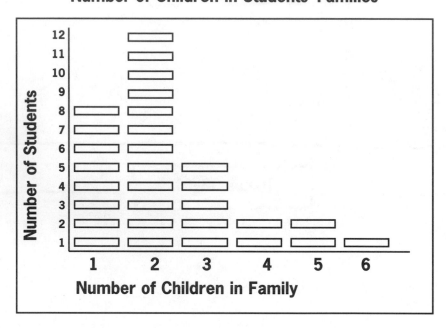

Look at the chart carefully. Then answer these questions.

How many students come from families with exactly two children in them?

_____

How many students come from families with only one child? _____

Two students have families with exactly _____ children, and two

have families with exactly _____ children.

There are only five students with exactly _____ children in the family.

How many students are in this group? _____

Name _____

Fluency Builder

gravitational	tree	brighter
bulge	bird	sunlight
inlet	this	high
generated	hot	mighty
energy	over	night
shallow	fall	
	had	
	pull	
	come	

1. Krakatoa / was a peaceful place / with many birds, / trees, / and sunlight.

2. Then in 1883, / hot ash from Krakatoa / formed dark clouds / over the ocean, / turning daytime to night.

3. The red glow / over the volcano / grew brighter. / The ocean began / to rise and fall, / smashing the boats / in the inlet.

4. Earthquakes underwater / had generated a tsunami!

5. The tsunami didn't come / from the tidal bulge / made by the gravitational pull / of the moon.

6. It was powered / by the energy / of the earthquakes / started by the explosion / of Krakatoa.

7. The next day, / a new tsunami grew bigger and bigger / as it crossed the shallow waters / near the coastline.

8. The mighty wave / traveled around the world, / and even to this day, / people will never forget / that Krakatoa caused this to happen.

The Krakatoa Wave

Do what the sentences tell you to do.

1. It is nighttime. Make the skies dark.
2. Inside, Dwight tries to fix his bike seat. Add a seat to his bike.
3. Dwight's sight is not good. Give him glasses so he can do his work.
4. Dwight must put a bright reflector on the seat of his bike. Put the round reflector in his hand.
5. Dwight has put the bike light on backward. Cross out the light, and sketch it the right way.
6. It is not very bright in here. Add a new light bulb.
7. Mom tries to reach a box, but it is too high. Make a ladder for her.
8. She will need a flashlight to see inside the box. Give her one.
9. Dad has pried open a sealed box. Sketch what is inside.
10. Dad's shoelace has come untied. Draw an untied shoelace on his right shoe.
11. Flick, the cat, cries for a toy. Make a tennis ball for Flick to play with.
12. Flick is missing his spots! Add spots on his thighs and back.
13. Flick likes to lie on rugs. Make a rug for Flick to lie on.
14. Flick is frightened by a bee that flies by. Draw the bee.

Now circle all the words that have the /ī/ sound spelled *igh* or *ie*.

Harcourt

The Krakatoa Wave

Complete the sequence chart about
"The Krakatoa Wave." Write a
sentence in each box. The
first one is done for you.

Event 1:

Krakatoa exploded on August 26, 1883.

Event 2:

Event 3:

Event 4:

Now use the information from the boxes to write a one-sentence summary of
the selection.

_____

_____

Harcourt

Text Structure: Main Idea and Details

Read this paragraph.

Not too many people live near active volcanoes. Everyone, however, might some day experience a natural disaster. It could be a flood, a tornado, a hurricane, or an earthquake. In order to stay safe, the most important thing is to pay attention. Radio or television reports will probably tell you if there is a possible disaster. If you are in an area of danger, you may have to leave. It is important to leave immediately if police or other officials tell you to. Don't worry about your things. Your safety is more important than anything you own.

Read the paragraph again. Decide if each sentence is part of the main idea (MI) or the supporting details (SD). Below, label each sentence with either MI or SD.

Not too many people live near active volcanoes. _____

Everyone, however, might some day experience a natural disaster. _____

It could be a flood, a tornado, a hurricane, or an earthquake. _____

In order to stay safe, the most important thing is to pay attention. _____

Radio or television reports will probably tell you if there is a possible disaster. _____

If you are in an area of danger, you may have to leave. _____

It is important to leave immediately if police or other officials tell you to. _____

Don't worry about your things. _____

Your safety is more important than anything you own. _____

Write the main idea of this paragraph in your own words.

_____

Fluency Builder

sensors	found	edge
reef	around	ridges
lagoon	animal	gently
atoll	grow	largest
barren	between	
meander	floor	
	when	
	sea	
	years	
	without	

1. Coral reefs are found / in oceans / around the world.

2. Each tube-shaped coral animal / has a mouth / surrounded by fingerlike sensors.

3. Some reefs grow / around the edge / of a volcanic island.

4. When water flows / between an ancient volcano / in the ocean floor and a reef, / a calm lagoon is formed.

5. An atoll is created / when the ancient volcano disappears.

6. Sea animals meander / in and out of coral gardens / in the Great Barrier Reef, / the largest on Earth.

7. A coral reef grows very slowly— / its ridges may be only 3 feet higher in 1,000 years.

8. Without sunlight / and gently moving water, / coral reefs would become / barren piles of rock.

Name _____

Gardens of the Sea: Coral Reefs

Read the story. Circle all the words that have the sound the letter g stands for in the word general.

The giant giraffe wanted to drink some water. She walked slowly to the edge of the lake.

At the same time, a villager crossed the bridge. He wanted to fill his large bucket with water for his vegetables.

Neither the giraffe nor the villager saw the danger lurking in the hedges. Then a strange sound made them both look up.

A huge cat came flying out of the hedge. It was the largest beast the villager had ever seen. The villager flew like a gymnast into a tree. The giraffe turned and ran over the ridge.

Luckily, wildlife biologists also heard the sound. They trapped the cat in a cage. Then they drove it far away from the village and the lake.

Circle and write the word that best completes each sentence.

1. The giant _____ was thirsty.
         giraffe   gerbil   hedgehog

2. A villager needed water for his _____.
                 vegetables   pages   fringe

3. A huge cat was hiding behind the _____.
               hedge   slug   ginger

4. Neither the giraffe nor the man saw the _____.
             gem   engine   danger

5. Some wildlife _____ trapped the cat in a cage.
    geologists   biologists   badges

Gardens of the Sea: Coral Reefs

Write one or two sentences in each box below to show what you learned about coral reefs in "Gardens of the Sea: Coral Reefs."

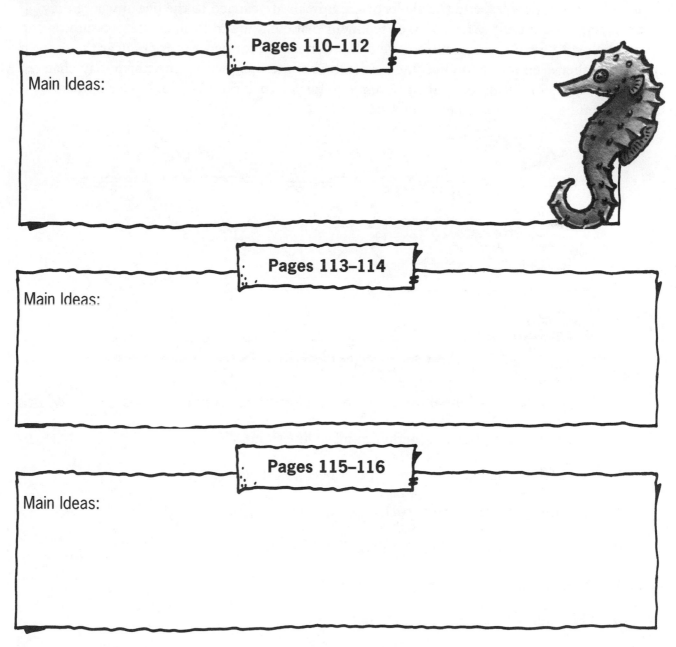

Pages 110–112

Main Ideas:

Pages 113–114

Main Ideas:

Pages 115–116

Main Ideas:

Write a one-sentence summary statement about the selection.

_____

_____

Harcourt

Graphic Aids

Read the passsage and study the diagram to answer the questions.

Mud, clay, sand, pebbles, and the shells of sea animals are carried to the ocean where they form layers of sediment. The layers of sediment that continue to form create pressure on the layers below to form rock. As more layers of sediment are formed, the rocks near the bottom press together even more and become harder. Sometimes heat within the Earth may change the rocks, too. For example, mud compresses to form a rock called shale. Under more pressure and heat, the shale becomes slate.

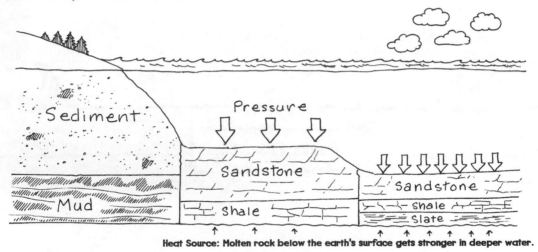

Heat Source: Molten rock below the earth's surface gets stronger in deeper water.

1. Which information in the illustration does the reading selection describe?

    a. Sea animals are pressed together to make limestone.

    b. As shale experiences more pressure, it becomes slate.

    c. Sandstone becomes a hard rock called quartz.

    d. Marble was once the skeletal remains of animals.

2. Which of these does the diagram explain?

    a. The layers of rock are changing due to pressure and heat.

    b. The sea animals live to be hundreds of years old.

    c. Some sand and mud can be carried to the ocean by the wind.

    d. Waves wash against the rocks and slowly break the rock into sand.

Harcourt

Fluency Builder

translation   made   space

publicity   paper   center

features   they   face

piercing   hungry   sincere

advanced   knew   slices

                  looks   celery

                  their   pencil

                  few

1. The space people advanced / on Miss Clancy / with piercing looks.

2. Miss Clancy made herself / calmly face them / in the center / of the gym.

3. She asked / if they wanted publicity / about their arrival.

4. The space people shook / their heads no, / and they seemed sincere.

5. From their features, / Vince knew / they were from Mars.

6. With paper and pencil, / they made marks / which looked / like a code.

7. After a few minutes, / Vince was able / to make a translation / of the markings.

8. The hungry space people / ate cheese slices / and celery sticks.

An Encounter with Space People

Circle and write the word that best completes each sentence.

1. Cathy is teaching Cyrus how to tap _____.

   dance   date   dark

2. Cathy has taken tap classes _____ she was six.

   skill   since   silence

3. Cyrus _____ to learn how to dance, too.

   decoded   decided   deduced

4. Cathy and Cyrus stand in the _____ of the hall. They wait for the music to begin.

   center   circle   cabin

5. They spin in _____ as they dance.

   collars   processes   circles

6. Cathy hopes to perform with Cyrus at the winter _____.

   center   concert   crowd

7. She circles the date in _____ on her calendar.

   pencil   purple   puzzle

8. On the big night, Cyrus and Cathy both wear _____ costumes.

   fancy   finally   finicky

9. When the dancing _____,

   causes   calls   ceases

   the people clap wildly.

10. After the concert, Cathy and Cyrus

    _____ their success.

    celery   career   celebrate

An Encounter with Space People

Complete the story map for "An Encounter with Space People."

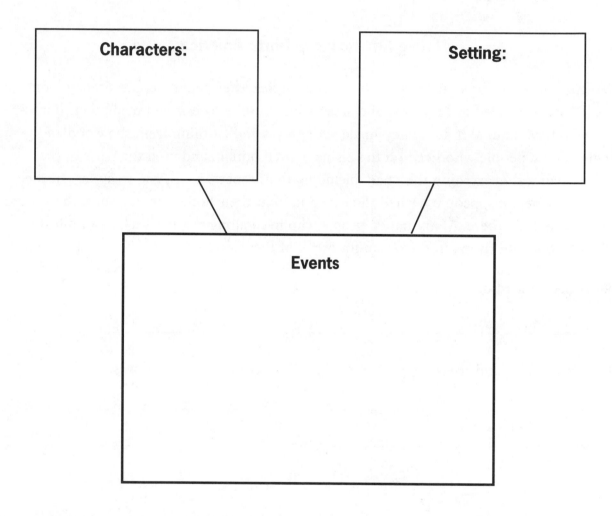

Characters:

Setting:

Events

Text Structure: Main Idea and Details

Read the passage. Then answer the question and complete this outline based on the passage.

Native Americans in North America

When European explorers first came to North America, they found people already living there. Those who lived in the woodland areas hunted in the forests and made their homes out of wood and animal hides. They made many tools and clothing from the woodland animals. Those people who lived on the plains hunted buffalo and used the parts of the buffalo for almost everything they had, including their tepees, tools, and weapons. In the southwestern regions, people farmed the land and built their homes of clay since there were no trees or buffalo there. Many native people who lived along the Pacific Coast built their homes of wood and fished in the ocean for much of their food.

What is the implied or suggested idea of this passage? _____

_____

I. People in woodland areas

    A. _____

    _____

    B. _____

    _____

II. _____

    A. hunted buffalo

    B. _____

    _____

III. People in the southwest

    A. _____

    B. _____

IV. _____

    A. _____

    B. _____

Harcourt

Fluency Builder

rations   their   Roy
homestead   step   choice
concocted   was   boil
perch   have   boy
undeniable when   enjoy
despair   get
            make
            pan
            you're

1. From their perch / on the porch steps, / Roy and Pearl looked / at the homestead.

2. It was Granny's birthday party / and they planned to have / an exciting weekend.

3. Much to their despair, / Roy and Pearl didn't have / a birthday gift for Granny!

4. Pearl suggested they make / a tasty pan of fudge.

5. Roy said, / "Good choice, / but you're looking / at a boy / who can't even boil water."

6. Roy brooded / about one undeniable fact; / they still had no present for Granny.

7. When Granny tasted the fudge / they had concocted, / they smiled.

8. When Granny was a girl, / sugar rations were precious, / and she didn't get to enjoy sweets / as often as she did now.

Name _____

Peppermint-Peanut-Butter Fudge

Write the word that answers each riddle.

1. I have the same vowel sound as in *boy*.

   You put me in a car's motor. What am I? _____

                                     oil   gas   owl

2. I have the same vowel sound as in *toy*.

   I live in the sea. What am I? _____

                         flounder   oyster   employee

3. I have the same vowel sound as in *joy*.

   You can pay for things with me. What am I? _____

                             coin   dollar   coil

4. I have the same vowel sound as in *boil*.

   You use me to speak. What am I? _____

                        choice   voice   mouth

5. My second syllable has the same vowel sound as in *loyal*.

   I am someone's boss. What am I? _____

                    enjoying   foreman   employer

6. I have the same vowel sound as in *join*.

   I am often loud. What am I? _____

                    sound   noise   poise

7. My first syllable has the same vowel sound as in *moist*.

   I am a king or queen. What am I? _____

                    royalty   loyalty   ruler

8. I have the same vowel sound as in *boys*.

   You can plant seeds in me. What am I? _____

                      ground   soil   foil

9. My second syllable has the same vowel sound as in *broil*.

   I mean "to bother." What word am I? _____

   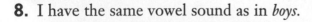

                    appoint   annoy   distract

Harcourt

Peppermint-Peanut-Butter Fudge

Complete the sequence chart for "Peppermint-Peanut-Butter Fudge." Write a sentence in each box. The first one has been done for you.

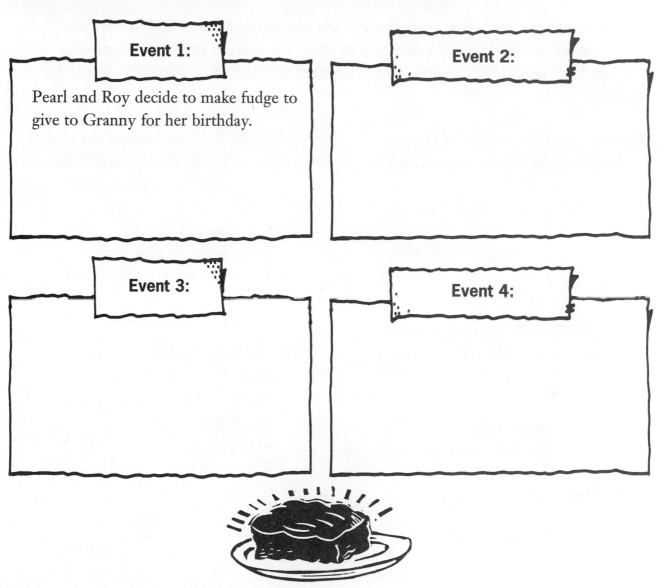

Event 1:

Pearl and Roy decide to make fudge to give to Granny for her birthday.

Event 2:

Event 3:

Event 4:

Now use the information from the boxes to write a one-sentence summary of the selection.

_____

_____

_____

Word Relationships

Multiple-meaning words are words that have more than one meaning. Use sentence and paragraph clues to decide the correct meaning of the word. Sometimes you can figure out the correct meaning by deciding the part of speech of the word.

Read the sentences below. Use clues in the sentences to choose the correct meaning for the underlined words. Read all of the answer choices before you choose an answer. On the lines, write the clue words that you used to select an answer.

1. Jessica is a key member of the team. She offers useful ideas for problems.
   A a low island
   B metal object used for unlocking
   C important
   D a part on a piano or typewriter

   _____

2. My friend and I will part company after dinner. I won't see him until he returns from vacation.
   A separate
   B actor's role in a play
   C a line where hair is combed in different directions
   D piece

   _____

3. We were all surprised by how far he could cast the ball. It landed halfway across the field.
   A a heavy bandage
   B throw
   C select actors for a play
   D a shade

   _____

4. When Alice received the bill in the mail, she paid it right away. She did not want her payment to be late.
   A a piece of paper money
   B a proposed law
   C the beak of a bird
   D a statement of money owed

   _____

5. Our large dog sleeps by the front door every night. It has been trained to guard the house from any intruders.
   A a shield
   B to protect
   C a player on a football team
   D ready

   _____

Harcourt

Name _____

Fluency Builder

congested	king	audiences
patron	plays	law
dismantle	many	applause
adornment	company	flaws
critical	they	faults
shareholder	family	haughty
lavish		taught

1. During the 1600s, / audiences were critical / of all dramas.

2. Molière was one / of four shareholders / in an acting company.

3. Molière's family / sent him to a college / to be taught law, / but he wanted to act.

4. They dismantled / their rolling stage in Paris / and performed / at congested theaters.

5. The king of France / became Molière's patron.

6. Molière based his plays / on the flaws and faults / of real people.

7. The king cherished Molière / as an adornment / to his court.

8. Many of Molière's plays / poked fun / at the haughty way / some rich people behaved.

9. Today / audiences still lavish / praise and applause / on Molière's plays.

Fluency Builder/Lesson 17 • Grade 5   **67**

A Man of the Theater

**Read the story. Then circle the letter of the answer that
makes each sentence below tell about the story.**

"Let's hurry up and finish lunch. Our show is starting," said
Saul. Saul and Dawn wanted to watch the new nature show on
TV. It had been launched only two weeks ago. It was a big success.

The first part of today's show was about wild birds. "Is that a
hawk?" asked Dawn.

"Yes," Saul said. "It saw a mouse and caught it with its claws.
Hawks have to work hard for their lunch."

The second part featured trout. "I didn't know some trout live in the sea," Saul said.

"The narrator said they have to travel to fresh water to spawn," Dawn explained. "It's a
long haul upstream to lay their eggs."

The last part was about deer. Saul said, "That fawn is eating plants near a lawn. Now it's
yawning. I guess deer feel sleepy after lunch, too. This show has taught me all sorts of things
about animals!"

1 What is today's nature show about?
  A how to make lunch
  B birds, trout, and deer
  C a mouse that catches a hawk
  D birds and insects

2 What did the hawk do?
  F It saw a rabbit.
  G It caught some lunch.
  H It landed on the lawn.
  J It crawled up a tree.

3 Why do trout swim upstream?
  A to launch a rocket
  B to haul a bale of straw
  C to cause a stir
  D to spawn

4 Where was the fawn?
  F on a seesaw
  G near someone's lawn
  H in a vault
  J in Saul's kitchen

5 What did the fawn do?
  A run across the lawn
  B draw a picture
  C yawn after eating
  D eat a prawn

6 What has the show done?
  F It has taught Saul about autumn.
  G It has shown astronauts.
  H It has told stories about authors.
  J It has taught Saul about animals.

A Man of the Theater

Complete the sequence chart about "A Man of the Theater." Write a sentence in each box.

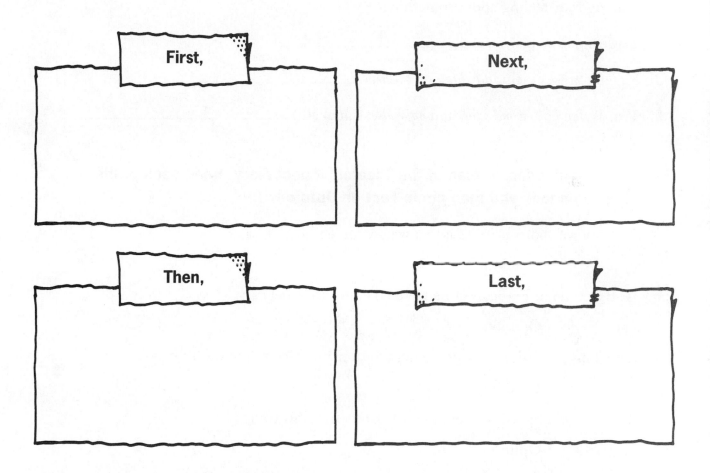

First,

Next,

Then,

Last,

Now use the information from the boxes to write a one-sentence summary of the entire selection.

_____

_____

Fact and Opinion

Read the sentences or phrases. In the blanks, write *fact* or *opinion*.

1. information that can be proven _____

2. a thought or feeling about something

   that cannot be proven _____

3. Signal phrases include *I think* or *I believe*. _____

4. Words like *best*, *wonderful*, and *enjoyable*, signal a(n) _____

Refer to the selection "A Man of the Theater" if necessary. Read each of the following sentences and then circle *Fact* or *Opinion*.

5. Molière was born in 1622 into a well-to-do family.

   Fact   Opinion

6. At that time in France, actors were no better than beggars.

   Fact   Opinion

7. The king gave Molière a permanent theater in which to put on his plays.

   Fact   Opinion

8. The king cherished Molière as an adornment to his court.

   Fact   Opinion

9. In 1680, the main theater in France was named "The House of Molière."

   Fact   Opinion

10. Since then, theaters everywhere have been congested with huge crowds when Molière's plays are performed.

    Fact   Opinion

Fluency Builder

illustrating	pictures	books
series	full	good
encouraged	box	wooden
pastels	teacher	could
charcoal	draw	would
	world	took
	very	
	when	
	began	

1. Istvan Banyai began drawing / when he was very young. / A good teacher / encouraged him to draw.

2. In his grandmother's house / there were wooden boxes / full of old photos.

3. He experimented / with charcoal and pastels, / but he always begins / in pencil.

4. When he draws, / he makes a series / of pictures.

5. Illustrating / is his job. / Pictures for one book / took Istvan Banyai / 120 hours to complete.

6. The light / inside the lantern / would flash onto the walls.

7. Using a pencil, / he could enter / an imaginary world.

8. Sometimes / he starts drawings / for a new book / by making dots.

My Imaginary World

**Read the story. Circle the words that have the vowel sound you hear in *took*
and *would*.**

Snook Stops a Crook!

Jenny owns a bookstore. Her cat, Snook,
comes with her each day to her job. Snook
likes to curl up in a peaceful nook in the
back corner. Shoppers at the store will stop
to look at the sleeping cat. "Would it be
okay to pet him?" they ask Jenny. "Yes!"
says Jenny with a smile. "He enjoys that!"

One day Snook helped catch a crook. A
man was looking at the cookbooks while
Jenny spoke with a customer. The man slid
a book under his woolen coat. He would
have left without paying for it, but he
bumped into the sleeping cat with his foot
by mistake. Snook sprang up surprised and
took off running. The crook couldn't stop
himself from tripping. He fell. The stolen
book slipped out. It landed on the wooden
steps.

After the police took the crook away,
Jenny hugged Snook. "What a good
cat you are!" she said. "You should get
a prize!"

Now write the circled word that best completes each sentence.

1. Jenny's cat, _____, comes to work with her each day.

2. Snook likes to curl up in a quiet _____ and sleep.

3. The cat once helped catch a _____.

4. The man was looking at _____ in the store.

5. When Jenny wasn't looking, he put a book under his _____ coat.

6. He _____ have left without paying for it, but he tripped over
the cat!

7. The police _____ the man away.

8. Jenny said her cat _____ get a prize!

Harcourt

My Imaginary World

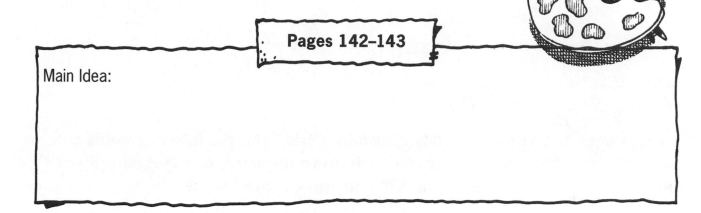

Write one or two sentences in each box to sum up what
each part of the story tells you about Istvan.

Pages 142–143

Main Idea:

Page 145

Main Idea:

Pages 146–147

Main Idea:

Write a one-sentence summary of the selection.

_____

_____

Harcourt

Word Relationships: Synonyms

Fill in the blanks.

A _____ is a word that has the same or nearly the same meaning as another word.

When you know the synonym of a word, you can figure out its

_____.

Look at page 145 in the story "My Imaginary World." Find the following words on page 145 and think of a synonym for each. Use a dictionary or a thesaurus if you need to. Check whether your choice of synonym will make sense.

drawing _____

good _____

scary _____

funny _____

different _____

developed _____

complete _____

Harcourt

Fluency Builder

pawnshop	sang	stoop
produce	near	music
errands	dance	new
numerous	star	afternoons
international	front	fool
gravelly	out	boost
	all	school

1. Ella lived / near a pawnshop / and a produce market / in New York City.

2. She sang / with her friends / on her front stoop / in the afternoons after school.

3. She could imitate the styles / of singers from the radio. / Some of their voices were smooth, / and some were gravelly.

4. When Ella was out running errands / with her friends, / they dared her / to enter a dance contest.

5. Her feet would not move, / so she had to do something / or look like a fool. / She sang.

6. Ella entered numerous contests / and won them all.

7. Ella Fitzgerald gave / her career a boost / by developing a new style / of singing called "scat." / She became / an international star.

With Love from Ella

Read the sentences and do what they tell you.

1. There is a ball in the pool. Draw the ball.
2. Give Andrew a hula hoop to play with.
3. Sue is holding a tool. Draw her tool.
4. Ruth has a bowl of stew. Draw her bowl.
5. Give Ruth a spoon, too.
6. Ruth's stool is missing. Draw a stool for her to sit on.
7. Sue has a cup of juice. Draw the cup.
8. Who threw a boot into the pool? Draw a boot in the water.
9. Andrew's swimsuit has stripes on it. Draw the stripes.
10. There are a few flowers blooming in the vase. Draw them there.
11. Andrew blew a big bubble with his gum. Draw the bubble.
12. A bird flew onto the roof. Put a bird there.
13. Draw a broom by the door.
14. The wind blew over a potted plant. Draw the plant coming out of the pot.
15. The plant's leaves are strewn around the pool. Draw a few leaves.

Now circle the words that have the long *oo* vowel sound.

Harcourt

With Love from Ella

Complete the sequence chart about "With Love from Ella." Write a sentence in each box. The first box has been done for you.

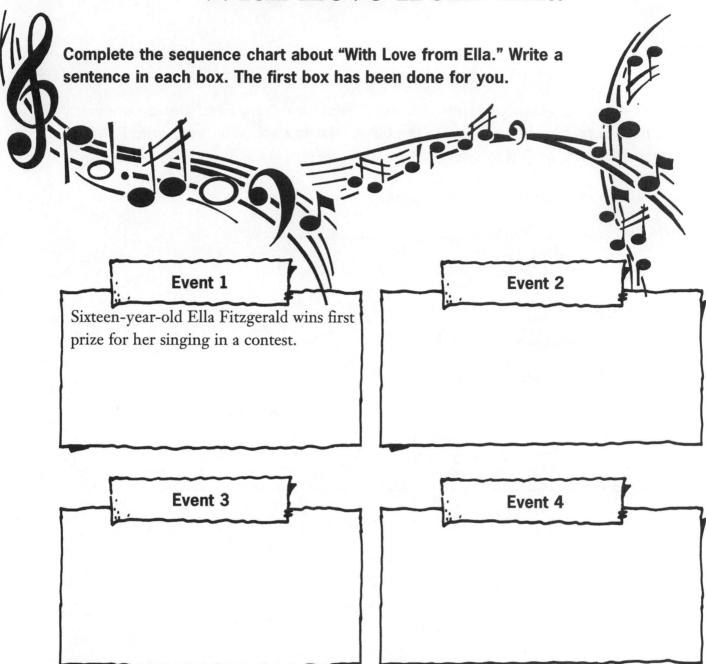

Event 1

Sixteen-year-old Ella Fitzgerald wins first prize for her singing in a contest.

Event 2

Event 3

Event 4

Now use the information from the boxes to write a one-sentence summary of the selection.

_____

_____

_____

Harcourt

Fact and Opinion

A **fact** is something that can be proved. An **opinion** is a belief not necessarily based on fact.

Read the following sentences from the story "With Love from Ella." Decide whether each one is a fact or an opinion. On the blank next to each sentence, write F if the sentence is a fact, or O if it is an opinion.

Chick was also a composer and he wrote numerous songs. _____

In 1938 I recorded one of them. _____

It was called "A-Tisket, A-Tasket." _____

It sold a million copies in only a couple of weeks and is still

one of my best-known songs. _____

When Chick died, I felt so blue. _____

I became the leader of our band and we played our music everywhere.

_____

The public loved us, as jazz was very popular. _____

After three years, however, I paused to consider my career. _____

It was time for me to leave the band and go solo. _____

Fluency Builder

migrant	**won**	**wrote**
timid	**full**	**wrapped**
flexibility	**days**	**wrong**
devote	**began**	**wriggled**
scholarship	**dance**	
thrived	**star**	
apprentice	**filled**	
	American	

1. The López family / migrated to Florida / from Cuba / when Lourdes was one year old.

2. While the clerk wrapped her shoes, / Lourdes wriggled her toes / into ballet shoes.

3. Lourdes devoted six days a week / to practicing ballet.

4. Lourdes won a full scholarship / to the School of American Ballet.

5. When she was 15, / Lourdes began her career / as an apprentice / with the New York City Ballet.

6. Lourdes was timid / when she first became a full member / of the New York City Ballet.

7. Lourdes didn't believe / she'd ever be a star, / but she was wrong.

8. Her life was filled / with hard work, / but she thrived on it.

9. Critics wrote / about Lourdes's flexibility / as a dancer.

Name _____

Lourdes López: Ballet Star

Circle and write the word that best completes each sentence.

1. Luke packed a sandwich, an apple, a soda, and a dog treat in his

   _____.

   knuckle   knapsack   freezer

2. He _____ to put a leash on Racer.

   kneeled   kneaded   begged

3. Racer was excited because he _____ they were going for a walk!

   knocked   knew   nabbed

4. They walked up a path that led to a grassy _____.

   knoll   knot   nest

5. At the top, Luke sat down and _____ his sandwich.

   unplugged   ordered   unwrapped

6. "I _____ you're hungry,

   know   knock   need

   too, boy," Luke told Racer.

7. "There are a lot of bugs out here, aren't there?" said

   Luke as he slapped at a _____.

   gnat   gnome   newt

8. It began to get cool, so Luke put on his _____ vest.

   knickers   never   knitted

9. As they walked home, Luke spotted a _____ on a tree branch.

   wren   wrist   runt

10. That night Luke _____ a letter

    wrapped   wrote   resisted

    to a friend about the nice spot he had found.

Harcourt

Lourdes López: Ballet Star

Complete the sequence chart about "Lourdes López: Ballet Star."
Write a sentence in each box. The first one has been done for you.

Event 1:

Lourdes López was born with a problem with her feet.

Event 2:

Event 3:

Event 4:

Now use the information from the boxes to write a one-sentence summary of the selection.

_____

_____

Text Structure: Main Idea and Details

The **main idea** of a piece of writing is what the selection or paragraph is about. It may or may not be stated directly. Details that give more information about the main idea are called **supporting details**.

Look back at the story "Lourdes López: Ballet Star." In each blank, write the main idea for the page given.

Main Idea, page 158

_____

Main Idea, page 159

_____

Main Idea, page 160

_____

Main Idea, page 163

_____

Main Idea, page 164

_____

What is the main idea for the whole selection?

_____

Fluency Builder

campaign	standing	laughed
residence	maybe	photo
obnoxious	chair	phrases
endorse	eye	emphasis
graffiti	I'll	geography
	front	Murphy
	some	
	ask	
	said	

1. During the campaign, / Al wore a T-shirt / with his photo on it.

2. A portrait of Lincoln / standing in front /of one of his residences / caught Murphy's eye.

3. Murphy thought / Al was acting obnoxious.

4. Murphy and several / other students erased / some graffiti / from the wall.

5. Al laughed / at Murphy's emphasis / on a campaign platform. / "Maybe I'll stand / on a chair / when I give my speech," / hc said.

6. Al asked the crossing guard / to endorse his campaign.

7. During geography, / Murphy heard whispered phrases / that included his name.

8. Al asked / the other students / to vote for the best candidate.

Certain Steps

Read the story. Circle all the words with the /f/ sound spelled *gh* or *ph*.

Phyllis and her father went to the zoo in Philadelphia. Phyllis is five years old. This was her first trip to the zoo. First they went to see the African elephants. The baby elephant trumpeted emphatically and made Phyllis laugh. Phyllis asked her father to take photos of it. She hoped to show the photographs to her brother Murphy. Then they went to see the giraffes. Phyllis thought they looked tall enough to reach the clouds! She asked her father to take photos of the giraffes, too. Then Phyllis asked the zookeeper to autograph the photo. Her emphasis on getting the autograph surprised her father.

"Why did you ask the zookeeper to sign the photo?" her father asked.

"That way Murphy will know the photos aren't phony," she said. Her response made her father laugh.

Circle and write the word that best completes each sentence.

1. Phyllis and her father visited the zoo in _____.

                    Pennsylvania   **Flowerville**   **Philadelphia**

2. Their first stop was to see the _____.

              graphs   **elephants**   **panthers**

3. Her father took lots of _____ of the baby elephant.

       photographs   **alphabets**   **autographs**

4. Phyllis wanted to show them to _____.

              Ralph   **Murphy**   **Philip**

5. She asked the zookeeper for an _____.

           alphabet   **elephant**   **autograph**

6. Phyllis made her father _____.

              talk   **laugh**   **frown**

Name _____

Certain Steps

Write a sentence or sentences in each box below to summarize the selection. Be sure to write the events in correct order.

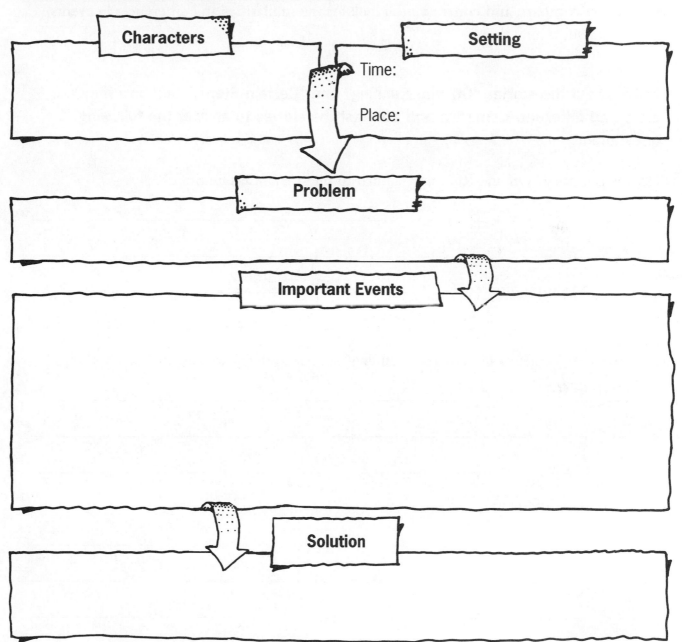

Now write a one-sentence summary of the story.

_____

_____

Text Structure: Compare and Contrast

When you **compare and contrast**, you look for the similarities and differences in events, characters, ideas, and things.

Think about the stories "Off and Running" and "Certain Steps," and how they are alike and different. Compare and contrast the stories to answer the following questions.

How is the story "Off and Running" similar to the story "Certain Steps"?

_____

_____

How are the stories different? _____

_____

How are the characters in "Off and Running" similar to the characters in "Certain Steps"?

_____

_____

_____

How are they different? _____

_____

_____

_____

Harcourt

Fluency Builder

polio	idea	threatened
decipher	some	instead
astonishment	who	spread
immobility	once	threat
dismay	many	dead
despised	believe	
	help	
	that	
	doctor	

1. At one time / some people who contracted polio / had to live a life of immobility / in an iron lung.

2. The spread of flu / once threatened people's lives.

3. Jonas Salk chose / to become a doctor / instead of a lawyer.

4. Dr. Salk's research required / a great deal of time / to decipher enormous amounts of data.

5. Dr. Salk hit many dead ends / before he finally discovered / a vaccine for polio.

6. Dr. Salk was astonished and dismayed / by his fame.

7. Dr. Salk despised the idea / of making money / from a vaccine needed to save lives.

8. Jonas Salk believed / that it is important for us / to do something / that helps humanity / as well as ourselves.

Quest for a Healthy World

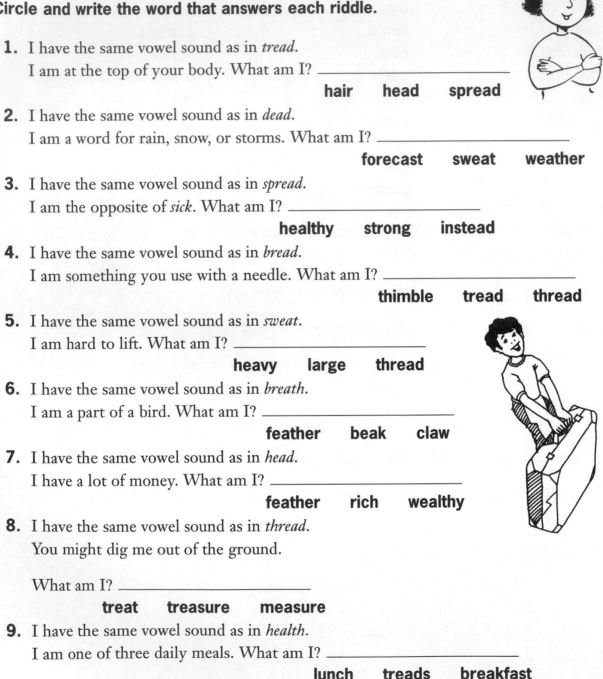

Circle and write the word that answers each riddle.

1. I have the same vowel sound as in *tread*.
   I am at the top of your body. What am I? _____

   hair   head   spread

2. I have the same vowel sound as in *dead*.
   I am a word for rain, snow, or storms. What am I? _____

   forecast   sweat   weather

3. I have the same vowel sound as in *spread*.
   I am the opposite of *sick*. What am I? _____

   healthy   strong   instead

4. I have the same vowel sound as in *bread*.
   I am something you use with a needle. What am I? _____

   thimble   tread   thread

5. I have the same vowel sound as in *sweat*.
   I am hard to lift. What am I? _____

   heavy   large   thread

6. I have the same vowel sound as in *breath*.
   I am a part of a bird. What am I? _____

   feather   beak   claw

7. I have the same vowel sound as in *head*.
   I have a lot of money. What am I? _____

   feather   rich   wealthy

8. I have the same vowel sound as in *thread*.
   You might dig me out of the ground.

   What am I? _____

   treat   treasure   measure

9. I have the same vowel sound as in *health*.
   I am one of three daily meals. What am I? _____

   lunch   treads   breakfast

10. I have the same vowel sound as in *deaf*.
    I am something you might do while jogging. What am I? _____

    sweat   eat   health

Harcourt

Quest for a Healthy World

Write one sentence in each box below to tell about Jonas Salk.

Pages 174–175

Main Idea:

Page 176

Main Idea:

Pages 177–178

Main Idea:

Pages 179–180

Main Idea:

Write a one-sentence summary statement about the selection.

_____

_____

Harcourt

Author's Purpose and Perspective

An **author's purpose** is the reason he or she writes the selection. The author's purpose can be to entertain, to inform, or to persuade. An **author's perspective** includes his or her opinions, attitudes, and feelings about the topic.

Look back at the story "Quest for a Healthy World." What do you think is the author's purpose for writing this selection?

_____

Here is a passage from the selection. Reread it and answer the question that follows.

Jonas Salk never applied for a patent on his polio vaccine. It would have made him rich, but he believed that such things must belong to humanity. There was a big hubbub among his peers, who said he could use the money for his research. It just seemed wrong to Dr. Salk. He despised the idea of making money from a vaccine needed to save lives. He would find other ways to raise money for his research.

What do you think are some of the author's opinions and ideas about Jonas Salk and medicine?

_____

_____

Look at the rest of the selection in your book. Write down two other attitudes or opinions you think the author has. What makes you think that?

_____

_____

Harcourt

Fluency Builder

insulated	noise	eight
muffle	cat	freight
partition	tried	veil
prowls	rope	weight
refinery	idea	break
grade	called	
submitted	around	
	would	

1. The loud noise / of the nearby refinery / did not wake Pete, nor did the early morning / freight train.

2. When Pete was asleep, / a mysterious veil / seemed to muffle all his senses.

3. "He wants to break his record," / Mark called out. / "He's been late / eight days in a row."

4. Pete was afraid / his grades would slip. / What could he do?

5. He insulated one wall / of his bedroom with blankets, / so his alarm would not / wake his grandma.

6. He tied a weight / to the end / of a rope. Pete tried to make / a cardboard partition / to fit around his bed.

7. Pete's cat / prowls the house / at night.

8. Pete submitted / his alarm / to the class invention fair.

9. "Now / that's what I call / an original idea!" / Mark called out.

Pete's Great Invention

Read the story. Then read each question. Decide which is the best answer. Circle the letter or statement for that answer.

Diana's neighbor Seth owns eight Great Danes. Great Danes are very large dogs. They can weigh up to 175 pounds! Seth's dogs can lick his face when they stand up on their hind legs.

Seth told Diana that together the dogs weighed more than a thousand pounds. After that Diana started calling the dogs the "heavyweights." Diana likes to tease Seth about his dogs. One day Seth told Diana that he feeds the dogs raw steak. Diana asked if the dogs' food had to be delivered by freight train.

At daybreak Seth takes his eight dogs for a walk. Diana likes to watch them from her window. She thinks the dogs' leashes look like reins. Once she told Seth that he should make fake antlers for his dogs. Then they could be his very own reindeer! "Seth driving a sleigh—how funny!" she said to herself. Seth didn't think it was such a great idea. It did make him laugh, however.

1 Who is Seth?
  A Diana's great-grandfather
  B a sleigh driver
  C a lightweight boxer
  D Diana's neighbor

2 What does Seth own?
  F eighteen Great Lakes
  G eight Great Danes
  H a freight train
  J eight reindeer

3 Why does Diana call the dogs the "heavyweights"?
  A They weigh eight tons.
  B They break sleighs.
  C Together, they weigh more than a thousand pounds.
  D They neigh like horses.

4 What does Seth feed the Great Danes?
  F chow mein
  G paperweights
  H reins
  J raw steak

5 Diana asked if the dogs' food is delivered by
  A a freight train.
  B a sleigh.
  C a neighbor.
  D a great supermarket.

6 When do the dogs go for a walk?
  F after a great meal
  G while unveiling a statue
  H at daybreak
  J every eight days

Harcourt

Pete's Great Invention

Complete the sequence chart about "Pete's Great Invention." Write a sentence in each box. The first one is done for you.

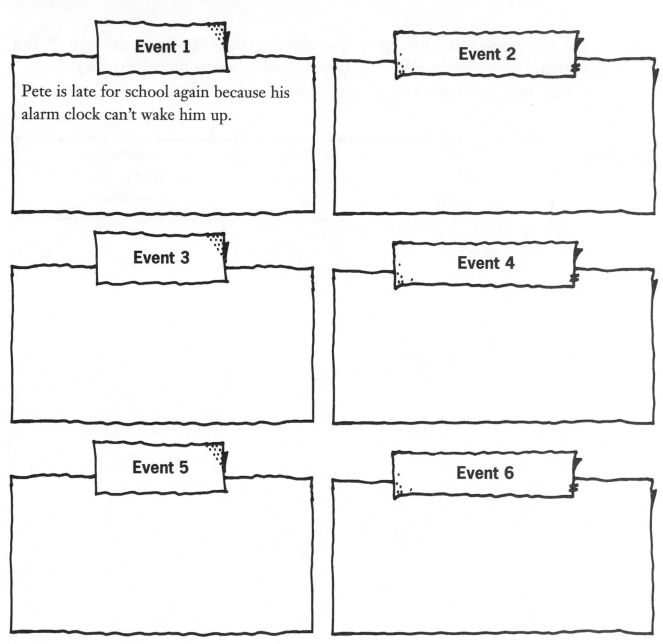

Event 1

Pete is late for school again because his alarm clock can't wake him up.

Event 2

Event 3

Event 4

Event 5

Event 6

Write a one-sentence summary statement about the selection.

_____

_____

Compare and Contrast

When you **compare and contrast**, you find similarities and differences. You can compare and contrast characters, places, events, objects, and ideas.

Think about Leigh and Pete, the main characters in "Dear Mr. Henshaw" and "Pete's Great Invention." Complete the Venn diagram to compare and contrast Leigh and Pete. You may use the words and phrases in the box to help you.

problem	noisy	boys	deadline
grandmother	writer	school	tardy
award	home	parents	invention

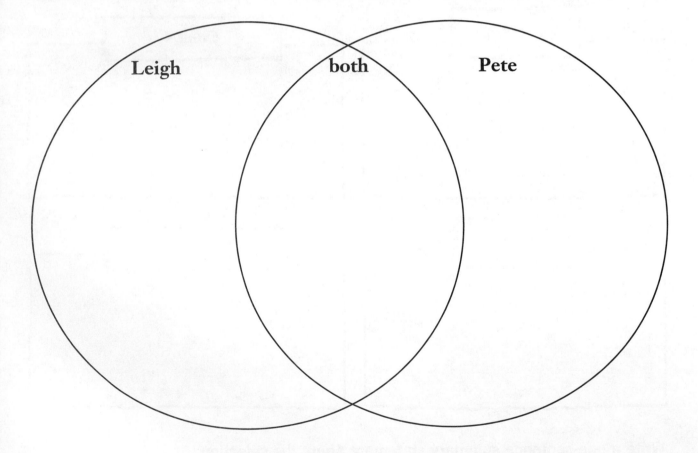

Leigh   both   Pete

Harcourt

Fluency Builder

beaming
reputation
sidetrack
absorbed
aisle
oath
word

guessed
first
board
would
when
anything
your
their

dumb
solemn
numb
column
comb
honor

1. The winners got points / added to their column / on the board.

2. Jenna's team could not let anything / sidetrack them. / Their reputation / and their honor / were at stake.

3. They took a solemn oath / to win the pizza.

4. First, / they would not / ask dumb questions.

5. Colin's team asked, / "Can you comb your hair / with it?"

6. Jenna was so absorbed / in listening to the questions, / that she dropped her kazoo / in the aisle.

7. Jenna was beaming / when she guessed / the correct answer.

8. The other teams / sat numb / with surprise.

One of a Kind

Read the sentences and do what they tell you.

1. Marty is sitting on a tree limb. Draw the limb he is sitting on.
2. Noni will climb the tree next. Add a rope to help her climb.
3. Marty is eating a cookie. Draw some crumbs falling from the cookie.
4. A lamb followed Noni and Marty to the tree. Give the lamb a name tag and a name.
5. Noni asks Marty if he reads her column in the class paper. Draw a speech balloon next to Noni, and write in her question.
6. Marty is honest. He says, "No." Draw a speech balloon next to Marty, and write "No" in it.
7. There is a beehive in the tree! Draw bees next to the honeycomb.
8. Noni sees the bees and whistles to Marty. Draw a whistle for her to use.
9. Marty is not listening. Put an X over his ear to show that he does not hear Noni.
10. A bee stings Marty's thumb. Draw the bee.
11. Noni feels bad that Marty got stung. She gives the thumbs-down signal. Draw it.
12. Marty does not cry often, but he starts to cry now. Draw tears on his face.

Now circle the words that have a silent *b*, *t*, *n*, or *h*.

Harcourt

One of a Kind

Write sentences in the boxes below to summarize the selection. Be sure to write the events in the correct order.

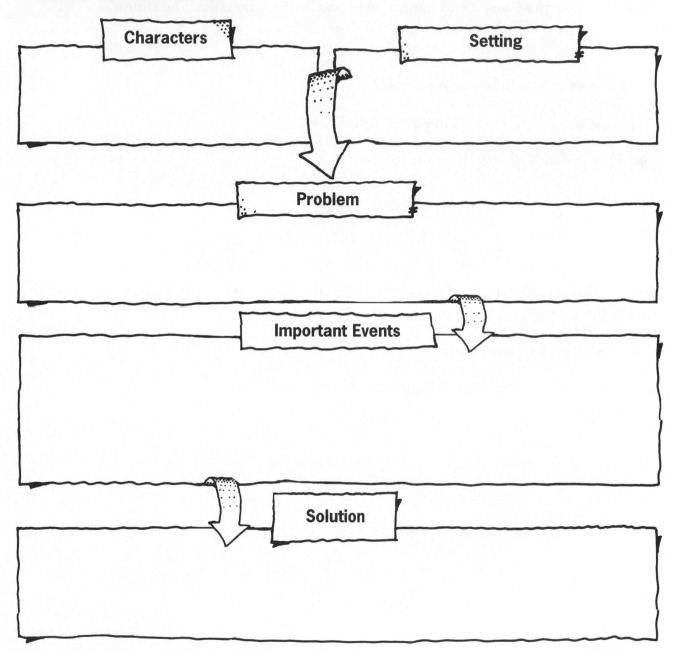

Characters

Setting

Problem

Important Events

Solution

Now write a one-sentence summary of the story.

_____

_____

Author's Purpose and Perspective

Read the paragraph. Then read the question and circle the correct answers.

An author's **purpose** may be to inform, to persuade or to entertain. The author's **perspective** includes the opinions and attitudes of the author.

What shows the author's perspective?

a. what the author chooses to put in the writing

b. how the author feels about the topic

c. the words used

d. all of the above

Answer the questions about the story "One of a Kind." Use your book if you need to. Circle the correct answer and fill in the blanks.

School should be very serious.

Does this represent the author's perspective?   Yes   No

What in the story makes you think that?

_____

_____

It is fun to use your mind.

Does this represent the author's perspective?   Yes   No

What in the story makes you think that?

_____

_____

Harcourt

Fluency Builder

sorrowfully	many	thoroughly
loftily	when	thought
dispute	found	tough
adjusted	talked	although
nonchalantly	called	
	once	
	they	
	how	
	said	
	knew	
	there	

1. There was a dispute / among the leaders.

2. Many were thoroughly scornful / of the Detroit project.

3. When jet tubes were invented, / people adjusted / to horizontal travel.

4. The diary writer found it tough / to get comfortable / in an automobile.

5. The manual talked loftily / about the wonders / of the convertible.

6. Solomon nonchalantly / broke into a shuffle / that he called dancing.

7. Although he once owned an automobile, / Solomon sorrowfully said / that it was not a convertible.

8. They thought / those people knew / how to have fun.

Harcourt

What a Time It Was!

Read the story, and circle all the words with *ough*.

Maya and Alden thought they saw something flash in a tree. "Look, it went through those branches," said Maya. "We ought to find out what it is." They could see the tiny object move through the leaves. Finally, the small blur got close enough to be identified.

Alden was thoroughly delighted. "It's a hummingbird!" he exclaimed. The bird was tiny, but it was as bright as a jewel.

The little bird zipped out of sight behind a branch. The children sought to find it among the leaves. "Tough luck," Maya said. "We lost sight of it."

"It must be rough to be so small in this gigantic world," said Alden. "I hope that little bird has enough to eat. Maybe we can help. We could put up the hummingbird feeder that my mom bought."

Maya and Alden brought the feeder with them on their next trip to the park.

Now write the word with *ough* that best completes each sentence.

1. Maya said they _____ to find out what the flash was.

2. The hummingbird _____ delighted Alden.

3. The hummingbird flew _____ the branches.

4. Maya thought it was _____ luck when they lost sight of the bird.

5. Alden thought it must be _____ to be so small.

6. Alden said he hoped the bird had _____ food.

7. Alden's mom had _____ a hummingbird feeder.

8. The friends _____ the feeder with them next time.

Harcourt

What a Time It Was!

Write one sentence in each box below describing what the diary writer discovered that day.

Monday

Tuesday

Wednesday

Thursday

Friday

Saturday

Sunday

Use the information in the chart to write a one-sentence summary of the selection.

_____

_____

Draw Conclusions

When we read, we can **draw conclusions**. We can draw conclusions from the words and actions of the characters, the information the author tells us directly, and what we know.

Read the following conclusions that could be drawn from reading the story "What a Time It Was!" What information in the story would lead one to each of the conclusions?

Conclusion: The diary writer didn't think much of the "old" automobiles.

_____

_____

_____

Conclusion: The diary writer discovered there were some good things about the old days.

_____

_____

_____

Conclusion: The diary writer had never seen a CD until Solomon played one.

_____

_____

_____

Harcourt

Fluency Builder

rigging
furl
huddled
vast
beams
lurked
settlement

world
wanted
would
sea
father
across
between
idea
because

disliked
unhappy
discouraged
unsafe

1. The voyage / of Christopher Columbus led / to the settlement / of the New World.

2. Manolo Sánchez wanted / to become a sailor. / His mother / disliked the idea.

3. Manolo was not discouraged / when the sailors / would tease him.

4. Manolo and his father / sailed with Columbus / across the vast blue sea.

5. One unhappy day / a terrible storm came up.

6. Water seeped / between the beams / and the wind ripped through the rigging.

7. Danger lurked everywhere, / so the sailors / huddled below the deck.

8. The crew furled the sails / because it would be unsafe / to leave them open.

Name _____

A Safe Harbor

Circle and write the word that best completes each sentence.

1. Alvin's mother was _____ when she saw his room.
   displayed   disproved   displeased

2. "I've been too busy _____ my bicycle to clean my room," Alvin
   said. **repackaging   reassembling   reconsidering**

3. "No more work on your bike until you _____ your belongings,"
   his mother said. **reorganize   reopen   replace**

4. "But that's _____!" Alvin cried. "I need to fix my bike so I can
   unfriendly   unwise   unfair

   ride with the bike club today!"

5. "Enough," said Alvin's mother. "When I _____ in one hour, your
   room had better be clean." **reappear   reconsider   remake**

6. Alvin sat down on his bed and stared

   at the mess _____.
   unavoidably   unhappily   uncontrollably

7. "You could start by _____
   restacking   releasing   redirecting
   your books on the shelves," said his sister Ella.

8. "Why are you being so helpful?" asked Alvin

   _____.

   unstoppably   unluckily   uncertainly

9. "I know how important it is to you to fix your bike so you can

   _____ the bike club," Ella explained.

   rejoin   replay   rejoice

10. "Boy, do I owe you one!" Alvin exclaimed as they started to

    _____ his toys.

    remodel   redesign   reorder

Harcourt

A Safe Harbor

Complete the sequence chart about "A Safe Harbor."
Write a sentence in each box. The first box has been
done for you.

Event 1

Manolo's father is hired as a cook on
Christopher Columbus's ship, and Manolo
gets to go on the trip to help out.

Event 2

Event 3

Event 4

Now use the information from the boxes to write a one-sentence summary of
the selection.

_____

_____

Name _____

Connotation/Denotation

The **denotation** of a word is its dictionary definition. The **connotation** of a word refers to additional feelings and ideas that the word suggests. A word may have positive or negative connotations.

Read the paragraph below.

One day a terrible storm came up. Waves nearly <u>flooded</u> the deck, and the ship tipped left and right, <u>struggling</u> to stay upright. Water seeping between the beams made us fear that the ship would sink. Danger from the storm <u>lurked</u> everywhere, but I tried to be <u>hopeful</u>.

Use a dictionary to write the denotation for each word below. Think about how the words are used in the paragraph. For each word, decide if the connotation is positive or negative. Circle the correct answer.

Flooded

Denotation _____

Connotation: Positive or Negative

Struggling

Denotation _____

Connotation: Positive or Negative

Lurked

Denotation _____

Connotation: Positive or Negative

Hopeful

Denotation _____

Connotation: Positive or Negative

Harcourt

Fluency Builder

guarantee	women	carefully
distinguished	stumps	assuredly
misleading	many	softly
indebted	their	thoughtful
interpreter	were	
suffrage	would	
anthem	says	
	could	
	group	
	right	

1. James and Lucretia Mott / were criticized for their views / on women's suffrage.

2. They could not guarantee / their distinguished guest's safety.

3. James says / that a thoughtful and just interpreter / would assuredly admit / his actions were right.

4. It would be misleading / to call the mystery guest / a celebrity.

5. Lucretia and Beth placed / bundles of food / on the tree stumps / by the woodshed.

6. Many escaped slaves were indebted / to the Underground Railroad.

7. The group joined hands / and softly sang the anthem, / "Free at Last."

8. Beth carefully / hid nearby.

Harcourt

Name _____

The Mystery Guest

Circle and write the word that answers each riddle.

1. You can wash me. What am I? _____

   washable   unwashable   watchful

2. I mean "full of color." What am I? _____

   uncolorful   coloring   colorful

3. You can easily get around me. What am I? _____

   avoidance   unavoidable   avoidable

4. I mean "in a way that is honest." What am I? _____

   honesty   honestly   dishonestly

5. I mean "without thought." What am I? _____

   thoughtful   thoughtless   thoughtfully

6. I mean "very sad." What am I? _____

   unsorrowful   sorrily   sorrowful

7. You enjoy having me around. What am I? _____

   enjoyable   joyless   unenjoyable

8. I mean "in a sad way." What am I? _____

   sad   sadly   saddle

9. I mean "without end." What am I? _____

   endless   ending   ended

10. I am filled with respect if I act this way. What am I? _____

    disrespectful   returned   respectful

Harcourt

Name _____

The Mystery Guest

Complete the sequence chart about "The Mystery Guest." Write a sentence in each box. The first one is done for you.

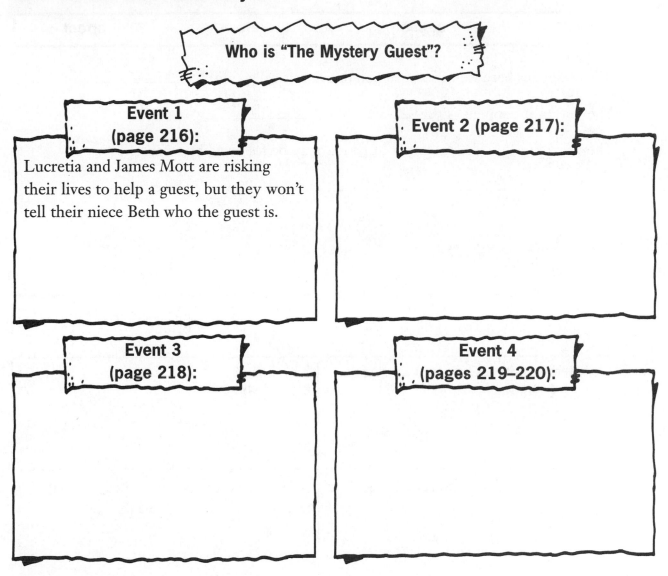

Who is "The Mystery Guest"?

Event 1 (page 216):

Lucretia and James Mott are risking their lives to help a guest, but they won't tell their niece Beth who the guest is.

Event 2 (page 217):

Event 3 (page 218):

Event 4 (pages 219–220):

Now use the information from the boxes to write a one-sentence summary of the play.

_____

_____

_____

Cause and Effect

Fill in the blanks with words from the box.

since	cause	therefore	effect

1. What happens because of some action or event is called a(n) _____.

2. The reason it happens is the _____.

3. The word _____ may be followed by a cause.

4. The word _____ may be followed by an effect.

Fill in the boxes.

Cause	Effect
Because Beth overhears her aunt and uncle talking about trouble,	
	As a result, Beth is sent to bed.
Because Beth sneaks outdoors when she is supposed to be in bed,	

Harcourt

Name _____

Fluency Builder

edition	worked	nonexistent
suspended	early	impossible
honors	almost	impractical
contraption	many	
repeal	first	
treaty	kite	
	his	
	their	
	was	
	chair	
	write	

1. In the early 1730s / novels were almost nonexistent / and nearly impossible to get.

2. Benjamin Franklin was the inventor / of many odd contraptions.

3. Franklin published the first edition / of *Poor Richard's Almanack* in 1733.

4. Ben Franklin suspended a key / from a kite / and proved / that lightning was electricity.

5. During his long life, / Franklin won many honors, / and worked on many / important matters.

6. Franklin got the British / to repeal some of their taxes / on the colonies.

7. After the colonies won their independence from England, / Benjamin Franklin helped write / the peace treaty.

8. Benjamin Franklin's inventions / included a rocking chair.

Who Was Poor Richard?

Read the story. Circle each word that has one of these prefixes: *im-*, *non-*, or *pre-*.

"Are you ready to go shopping for our party?" asks Tanya.

"Why are you so impatient to get started?" asks Luis.

"It's impractical to wait until the last minute," Tanya says. "That's why having a prepared list is such a good idea."

"Let's add prepackaged foods to the list," said Luis. "They are easy to preheat. They will be hot when the guests arrive."

"Nonsense!" snaps Tanya. "Home-cooked food is immeasurably better than the store-bought kind."

"Okay, you cook," replies Luis.

"Fine," says Tanya. "Now, should we order preprinted invitations? I think they might be too impersonal."

"It will be impossible to write them all by hand!" cries Luis. "We'd have to work nonstop for hours to make them!"

Circle and write the word that best completes each sentence.

1. Tanya and Luis have a _____ shopping list.

   prepared   previewed   prepaid

2. Tanya is _____ and wants to get going.

   impartial   impolite   impatient

3. Luis wants to add _____ foods to the list.

   predated   preheated   prepackaged

4. "_____," argues Tanya.

   nonstop   nonfiction   nonsense

5. "Should we send _____ invitations?" asks Tanya.

   presupposed   preprinted   prepackaged

6. Luis thinks it will be _____ to write the invitations all by hand.

   immobile   impossible   immaterial

Harcourt

Who Was Poor Richard?

Write one sentence in each box below to answer the questions. Use the page number listed as a guide.

Page 222

What were almanacs, and why were they popular in colonial America?

Page 223

How was Benjamin Franklin's almanac different from the rest?

Page 227

What is Benjamin Franklin also famous for?

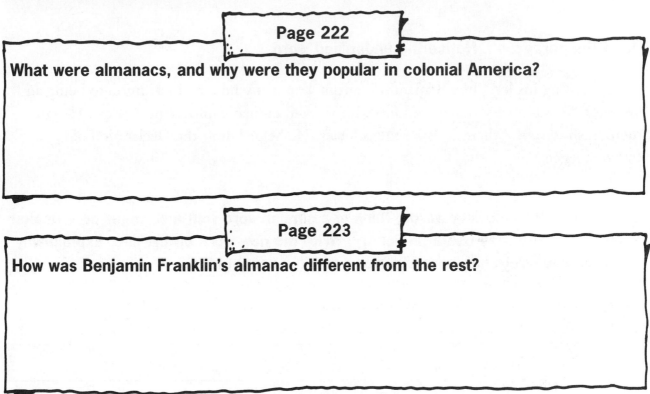

Write a one-sentence summary of the selection.

_____

_____

_____

Harcourt

Connotation/Denotation

The dictionary definition of a word is its **denotation**. The feelings and ideas connected to a word and its meaning are called the **connotation**.

Read the paragraph. Notice the underlined words.

During his long life, Benjamin Franklin won many honors. In addition to being an inventor, he was a very <u>skilled</u> diplomat. He <u>worked</u> on many <u>important</u> matters. He got the British to repeal their taxes on the colonies. He helped <u>draft</u> the Declaration of Independence.

For each of the following words, think of a similar word with a stronger or a weaker connotation You may use a dictionary. Write the new word on the line. Explain why the word you wrote has a stronger or a weaker connotation.

Skilled _____

_____

_____

Worked _____

_____

_____

Important _____

_____

_____

Harcourt

Fluency Builder

profusely	many	expedition
ordeal	ago	station
terrain	along	mission
dismal	that	invention
peril	first	completion
esteem	faster	
	was	
	had	

1. Expeditions of explorers / reached California long ago.

2. The distance mail had to travel / was great / and the terrain / was rough.

3. Carrying the mail by stagecoach / was a dismal ordeal / that took weeks. / There were many perils / along the mail route.

4. The mission of the pony express / was simple— / to get news and mail to / California quickly.

5. The job held in highest esteem / was that of rider.

6. A rider on horseback / rode from station / to station.

7. The completion / of the first pony express mission / took 10 days.

8. Bands played, / and a cheering crowd thanked the rider profusely.

9. The invention of the telegraph / in 1837 / provided a faster way / to send news.

Name_____

The Mission of the Pony Express

Circle the letter in front of the sentence that best describes the picture.

1 A Margaret uses caution when exploring.
B Margaret has a passion for the sea.
C Margaret visits the ranger station.

2 F She often takes vacations on her boat.
G She studies bird migration.
H She has a superstition about traveling.

3 A She planned an expedition down the coast.
B She wrote letters on her best stationery.
C She ignored the information.

4 F She followed the whale's migration.
G She worked for the coastal institution.
H She sailed to a far-off nation.

5 A She won the racing championship.
B Her face showed her happy emotions.
C Sometimes her boat was tossed by the waves.

6 F On occasion the waves were huge.
G She felt elation when the storm passed.
H She had to ration her supplies.

7 A In her opinion, sailing is boring.
B Margaret made it back in good condition.
C Margaret couldn't reach her destination.

Harcourt

Name _____

The Mission of the Pony Express

Write one sentence in each box below to show what you learned about the Pony Express.

Pages 230–231

How did news and mail get from the east coast to new settlers in California during the Gold Rush time?

Pages 232–233

What did a pony express rider do and who would take that job?

Pages 234–236

What happened to the pony express and its riders?

Now use the information in the boxes to write a one-sentence summary of the selection.

_____

_____

Harcourt

Name _____

Cause and Effect

Fill in the blanks.

1. The reason something happens is called a _____.

2. What happens as a result of an event or action is called the _____.

3. A cause can have only one effect. True or false? _____

4. An effect must have several causes. True or false? _____

Refer to the selection "The Mission of the Pony Express" to answer these questions.

The pony express first operated in April 1860. Write three causes for the formation of the pony express.

1. _____

_____

2. _____

_____

3. _____

_____

Write three of the effects caused by the start of the pony express.

1. _____

_____

2. _____

_____

3. _____

_____

Harcourt

Name_____

Fluency Builder

designated	first	attended
installment	hill	children
exodus	across	trustingly
migrated	they	capable
burrowed	take	expected
family	helper	impossible
years	enough	

1. Two years ago / the family migrated / across the plains / in the great exodus / from the East.

2. The family's first home was burrowed / into the side of a hill.

3. Each child has designated chores / to do every day.

4. Children living on farms / are expected to be / capable helpers.

5. When the snow comes, / it will be impossible / to get to the schoolhouse.

6. The family earned / enough money to pay / the first installment / on the loan / they had taken / for the land.

7. At the schoolhouse / children are playing / Snap-the-Whip.

8. One teacher taught / children of all ages / who attended the one-room sod schoolhouse.

Name _____

Frontier Children

Read the story. Then write the word from the story that best completes each sentence below it.

> April and Danny are taking a photography class. April wants to learn how to take better pictures of wildflowers. Danny wants to learn how to develop his photos himself.
>
> Last weekend April and Danny practiced taking pictures. They took a picnic basket to a meadow near their neighborhood. "I can't wait to start!" said April. "I see several flowers I want to photograph."
>
> "I'm famished," said Danny. "I think I'll eat first and take photos later." He unpacked the picnic basket and began to munch on an apple.
>
> Meanwhile, April walked around the meadow, snapping pictures nonstop. She did her best to remain motionless when she took each one, as her teacher had showed her. By the time Danny joined her, she had already gone through two rolls of film. "You're unbelievable!" Danny laughed when she showed him the rolls.
>
> "Not really," April said. "I'm just determined to improve!"

1. April and Danny are taking a _____ class.

2. They practiced taking photos last _____.

3. They went to a meadow near their _____.

4. When they got there, _____ started shooting pictures.

5. Danny was _____, so he chose to eat first.

6. The first thing he ate was an _____.

7. Meanwhile, April took pictures _____.

8. Danny thought she was _____ for working so hard.

Now draw a line between the syllables of each word you wrote.

Frontier Children

Write one sentence in each box below to show what you learned about frontier life.

Pages 238–239

What is life like for frontier children?

Pages 240–241

What challenges do newcomers to the frontier face?

Pages 242–243

What do the frontier children like about their new home?

Now use the information in the boxes to write a one-sentence summary of the selection.

_____

_____

Harcourt

Name _____

Summarize and Paraphrase

Fill in the blanks.

To summarize is to _____.

To paraphrase is to _____.

Read the following paragraph.

      At first the children yawn and blink sleepily. Outside their sod home, however, their energy is restored by the fresh air, and they shiver in the early-morning chill. Fall comes early in this climate, and soon the grass will be covered with snow.

Write a summary of the above paragraph.

_____

_____

_____

Read the following sentences.

The girl grabs a milk pail and a three-legged stool. Her designated chore is to milk the cow that waits in the small barn.

Write a paraphrase of the sentences above.

_____

_____

_____

Harcourt